180 Bible Verses to

EXPERIENCE PEACE

Carey Scott

180 Bible Verses to

EXPERIENCE PEACE

Devotions for Women

BARBOUR
PUBLISHING

© 2023 by Barbour Publishing, Inc.

Print ISBN 978-1-63609-641-4

Published by Barbour Publishing, Inc., 1810 Barbour Drive, Uhrichsville, Ohio 44683, www.barbourbooks.com

Our mission is to inspire the world with the life-changing message of the Bible.

Printed in China.

Introduction

Our ability to experience peace is a direct result of faith. The world may offer temporary fixes. They may tout options and remedies that at first glance look promising. But true peace comes directly from the Lord. And when you invest time in God's Word, your anxious heart will find peace.

The Bible is alive and active. While written thousands of years ago, it's relevant for every issue and struggle that face us today. From stress in relationships and fear of *what ifs* to apprehension from health challenges and concern over finances, peace can be experienced through the Lord.

Let God speak powerfully to you through His Word, bringing hope and help to your weary soul. And as you dig into scripture, peace will wash over you in supernatural ways. You will find rest. Your spirit will be calmed. Today, spend time with the Lord and let His presence melt the chill left by the trials and troubles of this world.

Pouring His Peace

Now, may the Lord himself, the Lord of peace, pour into you his peace in every circumstance and in every possible way. The Lord's tangible presence be with you all.

2 Thessalonians 3:16 TPT

Sometimes the only thing that will create peace in our heart is to ask God to literally pour it in. We've tried to manage disappointment in our own ways. We've reached for every earthly remedy we can find, hoping for relief. We've called on our friends and family, asking them to help us feel better. But even with our best laid plans, our stress level is still off the charts.

Friend, sit with the Lord today and let Him pour His peace into every circumstance and in every possible way. Living frazzled is no way to live. Ask God to show you peace in tangible ways so you can experience it right now.

No Fear in Troubled Times

*I have told you these things so that you
will be whole and at peace. In this world,
you will be plagued with times of trouble,
but you need not fear; I have triumphed
over this corrupt world order.*

JOHN 16:33 VOICE

We know the Word says we will have troubles, so expect them. We understand life won't be a cake walk. And we may even believe God is with us through the storms we're facing. But there are certain situations that knock us to our knees and make it hard to catch our breath, robbing us of every ounce of peace.

Let's remember that even in those times, God commands us to fear not. He has beaten this corrupt world once and for all through His Son, Jesus. And when we trust in Him for help and hope, it will be given in abundance. Peace will be restored.

Minds Trained on God

People with their minds set on you, you keep completely whole, steady on their feet, because they keep at it and don't quit. Depend on GOD and keep at it because in the LORD GOD you have a sure thing.

ISAIAH 26:3-4 MSG

- -

The most perfect and powerful way for us to stay in a position of peace is to keep our minds trained on the Lord. Doing so focuses our attention on Him so we don't toy with the *what if* thoughts that destabilize. It allows us to remain steady and steadfast, unmoved by the messiness of life. And we're able to persevere because our heart and mind are peaceful and trusting.

Train your thoughts to stay on God. It won't be easy when your world is shaken, but you can do it through faith. Be quick to pray and believe He will guide you through to the very end.

Being the Peacekeeper

"You're blessed when you can show people how to cooperate instead of compete or fight. That's when you discover who you really are, and your place in God's family."

MATTHEW 5:9 MSG

- -

There are times when it's up to you to keep the peace. You're the one who must stay calm in the chaos. You are who needs to be unoffended by someone's hurtful outburst. You must be the voice of reason when tensions run high. Your presence plays an important part in His plan. Yes friend, God may be asking you to be the peacekeeper.

When you seek His guidance, the Lord will walk you through difficult circumstances with strength. He'll empower you to facilitate cooperation and bridge the gap between others. And you will be a blessing to those around you as they watch you be Jesus. Even more, God will bless your obedience.

Making Your Life a Prayer

Make your life a prayer. And in the midst of everything be always giving thanks, for this is God's perfect plan for you in Christ Jesus.
1 Thessalonians 5:17–18 tpt

When you choose to make your life a prayer, it means you focus on living in ways that glorify God. You won't do it perfectly, but you will aim to live each day with purpose and passion. And in that pursuit, God will be central to every choice you make. In addition to sharing your heart with Him and asking for help, your prayers will be full of thanksgiving. Gratitude will spill over into every area of life.

Friend, the result of this kind of intentional living will be a heart full of peace. You will be immovable because your relationship with God will be unshakable. So let each day include the Lord and watch as your spirit stays steady in both the ups and downs of life.

Peace for the Taking

Peace I leave with you; My [own] peace I now give and bequeath to you. Not as the world gives do I give to you. Do not let your hearts be troubled, neither let them be afraid. [Stop allowing yourselves to be agitated and disturbed; and do not permit yourselves to be fearful and intimidated and cowardly and unsettled.]

JOHN 14:27 AMPC

What troubles your heart? Is it financial strain or a health challenge? Maybe you're struggling with being single or arguing more than usual in your marriage. Are you worried about your kids? Does the future cause anxiety? Is your career taking an unexpected turn? Is there fear that nothing will change? Scripture tells us to stop allowing ourselves to fall into these pits of despair.

Instead, consider that peace is available to you for the taking. It's been given by Jesus, and His peace is unmatched. What's keeping you from grabbing hold of it today?

Discovering Beauty

Don't hit back; discover beauty in everyone. If you've got it in you, get along with everybody. Don't insist on getting even; that's not for you to do. "I'll do the judging," says God. "I'll take care of it."
ROMANS 12:17–19 MSG

. . . .

Why would scripture tell us to discover beauty in everyone? If you think about it, it's hard to be at odds with someone when you see the good in them. When you learn to love their quirks, it's more difficult to sit in judgment. Rather than hit back, you're more inclined to extend grace and keep the peace.

So, make a concerted effort to find the goodness in those around you. Choose to overlook failings and faults. You're neither the judge nor the jury in anyone's life. No one is perfect—not even you. What a gift to choose to live peaceably as you accept differences in everyone around you.

Inner Calm

Let the peace of Christ [the inner calm of one who walks daily with Him] be the controlling factor in your hearts [deciding and settling questions that arise]. To this peace indeed you were called as members in one body [of believers]. And be thankful [to God always].

COLOSSIANS 3:15 AMP

With all the craziness of the world, it seems like a pie-in-the-sky dream that we could experience an inner calm. Our calendars are overpacked with family activities. Our days are filled with managing multiple projects, be it at home or the office. We must navigate challenging relationships that require every bit of patience we can muster. And rather than operate in that inner calm, we're stressed from walking in our own will and ways.

Today, ask God to help you prioritize peace. Let Him show you ways to let it be the deciding factor in your heart. Because if you don't, you'll miss out on the beautiful blessings that come from a daily walk with God.

Casting onto Him

*Casting the whole of your care [all your
anxieties, all your worries, all your concerns,
once and for all] on Him, for He cares for you
affectionately and cares about you watchfully.*
1 PETER 5:7 AMPC

When you feel worries start to creep in, cast them off you and onto God. Don't give them any time to stick. Don't entertain them or give them space to take root. Be mindful to not partner with them. Because when you embrace worry on any level, your peace will be ripped away. And rather than operating in faith, you'll begin operating in fear.

But friend, God's invitation to take away your worries stands anytime, day or night. No matter what is stirring you up, give it to God and experience His peace. He loves you. He is for you. And His plan for your life doesn't include wilting under the weight of spine-weakening and joy-draining anxiety. Be quick to give God anything that weighs you down and live in freedom and harmony.

Because of God

Now, because of you, Lord, I will lie down in peace and sleep comes at once, for no matter what happens, I will live unafraid!
PSALM 4:8 TPT

. . . .

Did you notice why the psalmist was able to lie down in peace and sleep? It wasn't because he put in extra hours at the office. It wasn't because he tried harder or burned the candle at both ends. It wasn't thanks to a new workout regimen or eating plan. And it wasn't a worldly solution to stress and worry. Instead, the psalmist gives all credit to God.

Let that be a powerful clue as to what will bring relief to you too. Regardless of the concerns stealing your peace today, God is the remedy. He's why you can stand unafraid no matter what life brings your way. And when you lean into Him for help through prayer, you'll experience peace and rest, just as the psalmist did.

Leaving It at His Feet

So here's what I've learned through it all: Leave all your cares and anxieties at the feet of the Lord, and measureless grace will strengthen you.

PSALM 55:22 TPT

. . . .

It's impossible to experience peace when we're carrying the weight of the world on our shoulders. Until we lay down all that causes anxiety, our heart will be stirred up and unsettled. And as believers, that's not the way we should be living. At some point, friend, we need to take hold of God's promise to handle those cares for us.

Let today be marked by your decision to experience His peace more than the stress of your problems. Choose to leave every worry, every fear, at the Lord's feet. They are not yours to manage on your own. Take Him up on His offer to lighten your burden, and exchange it for strength and peace and comfort. Those only come from God's grace.

Competitive Nature

*In every relationship be swift to choose peace
over competition, and run swiftly toward holiness,
for those who are not holy will not see the Lord.*
HEBREWS 12:14 TPT

. . . .

Are you competitive in nature? Do you like winning, some-times at all costs? Is it important for you to always be right? Does your desire to be the best or to be first often rear its ugly head? If so, you're not alone. And if we were honest, most of us would humbly admit to it. There may be a place for robust competition, but it's not in relationships.

Scripture says to be swift in choosing peace instead of conflict. We should adopt a servant's heart, leading us into a pursuit of holiness as we love others well. Can we have fun in games and take part in friendly competition? Yes, of course! But there's no place for serious rivalry with those we love.

Filled with Peace and Joy

*Oh! May the God of green hope fill you up
with joy, fill you up with peace, so that your
believing lives, filled with the life-giving energy
of the Holy Spirit, will brim over with hope!*
ROMANS 15:13 MSG

In those moments where you lack peace, ask God for it. When you need joy for the journey ahead, tell the Lord about it. These blessings are available to every believer at any time. Too often, we sit in our mess and feel helpless. We live with a feeling of hopelessness. And for whatever reason, we don't ask God to fill us up through His Holy Spirit.

The truth is that no matter what painful circumstances are weighing heavy on you today, peace and joy can coexist. Life can be difficult, and you can still have hope spilling over in your heart. And the key to living this way is an active faith.

Where Is Your Mind Focused?

A mind focused on the flesh is doomed to death, but a mind focused on the Spirit will find full life and complete peace.
ROMANS 8:6 VOICE

It matters where we focus our mind. Scripture supports that, saying one road of thought leads us to death while the other leads us to life. One allows us to rest while the other stirs us up. One path is combative while its opposite offers complete peace. And every day—sometimes every hour—we must choose which one to follow.

Think back over the past week. Has your heart been in a peaceful place, or have you been plagued with worry, fear, and insecurities? Has your mind been focused on fleshy things—desires and pitfalls of this world? Or have your thoughts been on faith things, like reading God's Word, praying with intentionality, and meditating on His goodness? Ask God to show you any changes that need to be made.

Go After Peace

*Let him turn away from wickedness and shun it,
and let him do right. Let him search for
peace (harmony; undisturbedness from fears,
agitating passions, and moral conflicts) and
seek it eagerly. [Do not merely desire peaceful
relations with God, with your fellowmen, and
with yourself, but pursue, go after them!]*

1 PETER 3:11 AMPC

- -

We're to go after peace. Rather than be passive and hopeful that peace will arrive, God wants us to pursue it with passion until it's reigning in our heart. Peace is something every believer should be asking for and moving toward daily. It's a blessing that is ours for the taking. Friend, are you going after it?

Don't let another chaotic situation derail you. Pray earnestly until you feel peace rush in. Be patient in the process, confident that God is good and in control. And be quick to give every fear and worry to the only one who can remove them.

Justified and Reconciled

*Therefore, since we have been justified
[that is, acquitted of sin, declared blameless
before God] by faith, [let us grasp the fact
that] we have peace with God [and the joy
of reconciliation with Him] through our Lord
Jesus Christ (the Messiah, the Anointed).*

ROMANS 5:1 AMP

Before you became a believer, you were at odds with God. But once you chose to accept Jesus as your Savior— recognizing Him as God's one and only Son who died for your sins and rose three days later—your faith ushered in peace. The cross reconciled you with the Father and declared you blameless in His sight.

While you will remain flawed this side of heaven, there is a powerful peace in your relationship with God. You will still mess up, but it doesn't change your status as *justified* before Him. Let that truth comfort your heart, especially in those sinful moments.

17

Peace from His Instructions

*The people who love your
Instruction enjoy peace—and lots
of it. There's no stumbling for them!*
PSALM 119:165 CEB

. . . .

Sometimes we don't like to be told what to do. We want things our way and on our timeline. We want our ideas to prevail. And we get agitated when we don't get to walk out the plan we decided was perfect. But living by faith means we set these selfish desires aside and instead choose to embrace God's will and way for our journey.

Consider the amazing sense of peace you could experience by simply following His lead. The Lord sees all and knows all, so obeying His instruction keeps your feet on the right path. It helps you avoid stumbling blocks to pride and selfishness. It deepens your faith as you surrender your will to His, and blessing will flow from it!

Actively Encouraging Goodwill

*And the seed whose fruit is righteousness
(spiritual maturity) is sown in peace by those
who make peace [by actively encouraging
goodwill between individuals].*

JAMES 3:18 AMP

We should be actively encouraging goodwill between us and others. Our heart should want a peaceful solution whenever possible, and we should take steps to make it so. But without God's strength and our spiritual maturity, it will be difficult to walk out well.

If you want to experience peace in your life, choose to live in deep community with the Lord. Every day, be intentional in pursuing righteousness. Focus on following God's will and ways. Because when you decide to make God's commands a priority and you nurture your relationship with Him in meaningful ways, you'll begin to crave the peace only He can provide. And it will overflow from your life and encourage others to live the same way.

Not a God of Confusion

When we worship the right way, God doesn't stir
us up into confusion; he brings us into harmony.
This goes for all the churches—no exceptions.

1 CORINTHIANS 14:33 MSG

God is a God of peace and order, not confusion and disorder. It doesn't matter where you apply this truth in your life, it stands firm. Whether in how you worship, how you share your testimony, or how you live your life each day, you can be certain that if confusion is present, it isn't from God.

Friend, in those moments, pray. Tell the Lord about your inability to discern the situation. Tell Him about your jumbled thoughts that feel overwhelming. Are you confused in a relationship? Are you unable to make sense of your finances? Are you looking at important documents you can't understand? Ask God for clarity in each situation, knowing He will clear the confusion and usher in reason and logic. And peace will follow.

Pray Instead

Don't fret or worry. Instead of worrying, pray. Let petitions and praises shape your worries into prayers, letting God know your concerns. Before you know it, a sense of God's wholeness, everything coming together for good, will come and settle you down. It's wonderful what happens when Christ displaces worry at the center of your life.

PHILIPPIANS 4:6-7 MSG

Prayer is the answer for anything you're facing today. Too often, we embrace an attitude of worry. We invite it in and keep it alive and active. We allow it to shift our focus away from our day, obsessing solely on all that could go wrong. But instead of entertaining it another minute, what if you chose to pray?

Scripture says that when you do, peace will overwhelm in the most wonderful ways. Choosing to let petitions and praises shape your worries as You talk to God will usher in calmness. His presence will settle your spirit and hope will return.

It Takes Practice

Do you want to live a long, good life, enjoying the beauty that fills each day? Then never speak a lie or allow wicked words to come from your mouth. Keep turning your back on every sin, and make "peace" your life motto. Practice being at peace with everyone.

PSALM 34:12–14 TPT

Notice today's scripture encourages us to *practice* peace. What a relief to know we aren't expected to understand the *hows* and *whys* right away. Just like anything else, it's a learning process. And with intentional repetition toward others, peace will take root. It will have a chance to become our life motto.

So, rehearse it in your relationships. Train through your interactions with coworkers. Make it a habit when you deal with strangers. Let it become a tradition as you parent. Make it part of your daily routine as you live a righteous life that glorifies God. What a gift to yourself and others.

The Fruit of Peace

But the fruit of the Spirit [the result of His presence within us] is love [unselfish concern for others], joy, [inner] peace, patience [not the ability to wait, but how we act while waiting], kindness, goodness, faithfulness, gentleness, self-control. Against such things there is no law.
GALATIANS 5:22–23 AMP

It's powerful to read about the fruit of the Spirit that believers have access to. There are such glorious benefits to allowing God to grow and mature your faith, so these blossom in your life. And one of the most wonderful blessings we receive is the fruit of peace.

With the world in turmoil and our hearts often restless, we need this now more than ever. There's just no good reason to let the weight of worry and fear sit on our shoulders. Life may be messy, but we don't have to be. Instead, we can thrive amid the chaos because we have inner peace that comes from God.

23

Good Choices

*When people make good choices, He is
pleased; He even causes their enemies
to live peacefully near them.*

PROVERBS 16:7 VOICE

. . . .

There are times it's hard to make a good choice. We know what we should choose, but our heart is pulled toward fleshy desires. There is a tension we must navigate. Our sinful nature rises up and demands its way. And rather than stand strong in our faith and trust God for the ability to choose wisely, we crumble under pressure.

But friend, every time we dig deep and make decisions that benefit us and glorify Him, God is pleased. Let that sink in a moment. Our good choices don't go unnoticed. God sees the grit it takes to override our preference for His perfection. He understands the sacrifice we make to remain faithful to His commands. And the Lord will bless every act of obedience with peace.

Blessed with Peace

The Lord will give [unyielding and impenetrable] strength to His people; the Lord will bless His people with peace.

PSALM 29:11 AMPC

. . . .

Think about how wonderful the gift of peace is to believers. We live in a fallen world where evil runs rampant. What's right is now wrong, and what's wrong is now considered right. We face bad news and challenging situations every day. We're bombarded by what the world considers valuable and important. And most of the time, these things do not honor or glorify God.

So to know that God will bless us with peace when we ask is a breath of fresh air. It's how we navigate the ups and downs of life. It's how we rest in Him instead of being shaken when trouble comes our way. And whenever we need His comfort and calmness to make it through hard moments, He will supply both in abundance.

An Advocate for Peace

*Deceit darkens the hearts of those who
plot evil, but advocates of peace have joy.*
PROVERBS 12:20 VOICE

There is a connection between peace and joy, and it's hard to have one without the other. Joy is a deep emotion fueled by faith. And being in a peaceful place because of God's presence allows that joy to rise up. No matter what difficult circumstance is happening in your life right now, when you trust Him for the remedy, it will calm your anxious heart and clear the path for joy to freely flow.

Friend, where do you need to be an advocate for peace in your life today? Is it in your marriage or as you parent? Maybe it's with a frustrating situation at work. Are you struggling with aging parents? Is there division in your church family? Are there issues with feuding neighbors? Or maybe it's in your own thought life. Choose to promote peace and watch joy begin to flood your heart again.

A Peace-Promoting Community

*When God reigns, the order of the day
is redeeming justice, true peace, and joy
made possible by the Holy Spirit. . . .
Join us, and pursue a life that creates peace
and builds up our brothers and sisters.*
ROMANS 14:17, 19 VOICE

Be encouraged that life won't always be like this. Right now, we're in a fallen world full of fallen people trying to figure things out. Scripture reminds us that Satan is the prince of this world, giving evil a chance to flourish. And too often, we can see evil infiltrating our lives and wreaking havoc. Without God, we are deeply misguided.

But when we pursue a life with others in a community where God is at the center, it's different. We see justice in action. We experience peace in its truest form. And His Spirit brings abundant joy. Even in dark times, we can allow the Lord to reign in our lives. We can create a peaceful space to encourage others to grow.

Paying Closer Attention

Finally, brothers and sisters, keep rejoicing and repair whatever is broken. Encourage each other, think as one, and live at peace; and God, the Author of love and peace, will remain with you.

2 CORINTHIANS 13:11 VOICE

- -

When God mentions something once or twice in His Word, we should definitely take notice. But when a command appears as often as *live at peace* does, we need to pay closer attention. It's so important to God. And that's why He says it more often.

What keeps you from living at peace with others? Is it a desire to be right? Do certain people exhaust you? Are you too cantankerous? Are there unrealistic expectations involved? Is unforgiveness an issue? Is pride in the way? Today, ask God to help you remove any barriers keeping you from living at peace. And then choose to glorify God through how you live out each day in community.

It's Going to Be Okay

See, God has come to rescue me; I will trust in Him and not be afraid, for the Eternal, indeed, the Eternal is my strength and my song. My very own God has rescued me.

ISAIAH 12:2 VOICE

There's a peace that settles over us as we realize we're going to be okay. Knowing everything will work out and we'll come through intact steadies our heart. In the moment, we may be frazzled and afraid. We may feel overwhelmed by stress and anxious thoughts. But as we remember God's promise to rescue us, those emotions will melt away.

Friend, peace is available to you right now. Even with all the hardships happening in your life, peace is yours for the taking. Peace will begin trickling in once you let Him be your strength and song. And as you unload every burden onto God, there will be a beautiful calm that will overtake you.

Prince of Peace

*Hope of all hopes, dream of our dreams,
a child is born, sweet-breathed; a son is given
to us: a living gift. And even now, with tiny
features and dewy hair, He is great. The power
of leadership, and the weight of authority, will
rest on His shoulders. His name? His name
we'll know in many ways—He will be called
Wonderful Counselor, Mighty God, Dear
Father everlasting, ever-present never-failing,
Master of Wholeness, Prince of Peace.*

ISAIAH 9:6 VOICE

Jesus has many names, all of which are full of power and reveal His awesome nature. But the name that sometimes resonates the very most is Prince of peace. Why? Because peace is often what we need the most. It's elusive. And it's not something we can create on our own. We may be able to calm ourselves for a bit, but it's not sustainable.

As a believer, you can experience peace through Jesus. Let Him be the one who settles your anxious heart.

Covenant of Peace

*For though the mountains should depart
and the hills be shaken or removed, yet
My love and kindness shall not depart
from you, nor shall My covenant of peace
and completeness be removed, says the
Lord, Who has compassion on you.*
ISAIAH 54:10 AMPC

God's love for believers is so deep that He makes a covenant of peace with you—meaning His love will never go away. Just as He promised Noah to never destroy the earth in a flood again, this everlasting covenant is just as real. And while in our humanity we will break it from time to time, God will never break His steadfast love.

You can't sin too much to make Him break His promise, friend. When you make bad choices and repent, there's nothing that will keep you from His presence. And it's in that sweet presence you will experience God's powerful peace and immeasurable love. It's available whenever you need it.

God's Wisdom

*But the wisdom from above is first of all
pure (undefiled); then it is peace-loving,
courteous (considerate, gentle). [It is willing
to] yield to reason, full of compassion
and good fruits; it is wholehearted and
straightforward, impartial and unfeigned (free
from doubts, wavering, and insincerity).*
JAMES 3:17 AMPC

God's wisdom is peaceful, proper, perfect, and pure. When
you ask for help, this is what you can expect to receive from
Him every time, without fail. Scripture says it's also full
of compassion. His wisdom will consistently be straightforward, unwavering, and considerate. This means His will
in your life is trustworthy on every level.

Too often, the wisdom we give or get from others isn't
peace loving. It's full of selfish desires, clouded by past
experiences. It's insincere, loaded with improper motives.
So, when you're asking God for guidance, make sure what
you think you hear aligns with His Word.

Inheriting a Blessing

*Don't pay back evil for evil or insult for insult.
Instead, give blessing in return. You were
called to do this so that you might inherit a
blessing. For those who want to love life and
see good days should keep their tongue from
evil speaking and their lips from speaking lies.*

1 PETER 3:9–10 CEB

Chances are you've spoken hurtful things to others. You've probably lied and insulted those you deeply care about. But God doesn't want you to live this way. Community is meant to be a place of encouragement and compassion. And when we abuse it in any way, He is not pleased.

The Lord's desire is that we instead choose to live in peace with one another. And while this may be a challenge at times, when we do it allows us to inherit a blessing. It sets us up to love life and see good days. It allows us to thrive in our relationships with others.

God Speaks Peace over Us

*I will hear what the True God—the Eternal—
will say, for He will speak peace over His
people, peace over those who faithfully
follow Him, [but do not let them abuse
His gift and return to foolish ways].*

PSALM 85:8 VOICE

What an honor and privilege to know God speaks peace over us. The one who created the heavens and earth, and everything in between, takes the time to say a pointed blessing over those who love Him. His words create with passion and purpose. And there is no one else whose words matter more.

So, starting today, let us decide we want to be women who recognize this gift and respond accordingly. Let us be faithful, choosing to live righteously as we wake each morning. Let us bask in the peace He freely provides. It's when our heart is full of love for God that the desire to follow His will and ways grows.

Unpack It All with God

Relax, everything's going to be all right;
rest, everything's coming together;
open your hearts, love is on the way!
JUDE 2:2 MSG

Friend, everything is going to work out. It may not feel that way right now, but all the stress you're experiencing will melt away. The anxiety you are struggling to manage will eventually calm down. And yes, every detail will come together in the end. But until then, let God bring peace to your heart.

Right now, go to God in prayer. Tell Him the full spectrum of what's burdening your heart. Unpack everything that concerns you. Share the apprehension that keeps you up at night. Talk to Him about the fears that preoccupy your mind during the day. Pour it all out, and then watch as God's peace begins to settle into those places. Let God love you in meaningful ways as You benefit from the comfort of His presence.

The Breaking That Made Us Whole

Yet it was our suffering he carried, our pain
and distress, our sick-to-the-soul-ness.
We just figured that God had rejected him,
that God was the reason he hurt so badly.
But he was hurt because of us; he suffered so.
Our wrongdoing wounded and crushed him.
He endured the breaking that made us whole.
The injuries he suffered became our healing.

ISAIAH 53:4–5 VOICE

Knowing what Jesus suffered and endured on the cross to set us free from the price of sin, we simply can't ignore the peace it bought. He carried our suffering. He hurt because of us. It was our sin that crushed Him. So, when we choose to stay stirred up and stressed out, we aren't appreciating that His injuries became our healing.

Friend, grab onto the peace He affords you. Don't sit in fear and anxiety a minute longer. Jesus made you whole. Embrace it with all you have.

How to Conduct Yourself

Conduct yourselves with all humility, gentleness, and patience. Accept each other with love, and make an effort to preserve the unity of the Spirit with the peace that ties you together. You are one body and one spirit, just as God also called you in one hope.

EPHESIANS 4:2-4 CEB

The Word talks so often about the importance of working together in community. God wants us to be peacemakers and peacekeepers whenever possible. Think about it. When we are at odds with others, it weakens our witness. It keeps us preoccupied with drama so we're ineffective in divine work. And it can easily embitter our heart, hardening it toward the church or people we interact with regularly.

If you want to consistently experience peace in life, then decide to live out today's verse with passion. It will please God, and it will soften your heart toward others, drawing them close to you in love and hope.

Still the Beneficiaries

Then all at once in the night sky, a vast
number of glorious angels appeared, the
very armies of heaven! And they all praised
God, singing: "Glory to God in the highest
realms of heaven! For there is peace and
a good hope given to the sons of men."

LUKE 2:13–14 TPT

Can you even imagine this angelic sighting by hard-working shepherds tending to their flocks? What a powerful and profound way to announce Jesus' birth! And then to hear their singing fill the night sky, proclaiming peace and hope has arrived. Simply beautiful.

We may have missed this epic display, but we are still the beneficiaries of every good gift Jesus' life and death provided. As believers, we can grab onto hope every day. We can let peace reign in our heart always. And because of that, we can praise and sing our gratitude to God for all He has done for us.

Messengers of Peace

How beautiful upon the mountains are the feet of a messenger who proclaims peace, who brings good news, who proclaims salvation, who says to Zion, "Your God rules!" Listen! Your lookouts lift their voice; they sing out together! Right before their eyes they see the LORD returning to Zion.

ISAIAH 52:7-8 CEB

Every day, you can be a messenger who proclaims peace and reminds others that God is good! By the way you live and the words you speak, you can encourage those around you with good news. What's keeping you from it?

Ask God to open your eyes to opportunities. Ask Him to open doors at the right time, so you can share His goodness where it's desperately needed. Help others experience the peace of Jesus. Be always ready to share your testimony as well as powerful God-moments with the hopeless. Look for ways to create community so you can encourage each other that God rules and reigns and will return again soon!

His Ways and Thoughts Are Higher

*"For My thoughts are not your thoughts,
nor are your ways My ways," declares the
LORD. "For as the heavens are higher than the
earth, so are My ways higher than your ways
and My thoughts higher than your thoughts."*

ISAIAH 55:8-9 AMP

When you think about it, if God's thoughts and ways were like ours, it would make Him common. If we were able to figure Him out because we thought alike, it would remove His mystery. It may frustrate us from time to time, but God's sovereignty is a gift in and of itself. Who would want to serve a god without divinity?

Knowing this reality should settle your anxious heart a bit. You don't have to figure everything out because He will. He has. And that means you can relinquish control over all your stresses and struggles, choosing to trust God is straightening your crooked paths in His infinite wisdom and power.

Righteousness Yields Peace

So it will be until God pours out the Spirit from up above, and the land comes alive again—desert to fertile field, fertile field to forest. Then justice and truth will settle in the desert places, and righteousness will infuse the fertile land. Then righteousness will yield peace, and the quiet and confidence that attend righteousness will be present forever.

Isaiah 32:15-17 voice

Even though Israel broke their covenant with God, He didn't break His covenant with them. He continued to love them unconditionally. And while they had to walk out the natural consequences of their sin, God promised to bring them back into a right relationship with Him. He restored peace and righteousness.

Your life may be a mess right now, but Jesus is the King of righteousness. His work on the cross brings peace with God to all believers. And in His great love, He promises to fill hearts with peace, for those who walk in spirit and truth. Let that be you.

Out of Captivity

For you will go out in joy, be led home in peace. And as you go the land itself will break out in cheers; the mountains and the hills will erupt in song, and the trees of the field will clap their hands.

ISAIAH 55:12 VOICE

This verse is talking about the Jews' release from captivity and the return to their own land. And notice they are accompanied by joy and peace. But friend, we can connect to the deeper meaning of this passage of scripture when we look at our own redemption.

When you became a believer, you were released from your bondage to sin. You left the pit of agony and distress. And you took the hand of God as He led you to where you can experience the Lord's love, joy, and peace every day. Decide now to hold on tightly and never let go.

Let God Be God

Surrender your anxiety. Be still and realize that
I am God. I am God above all the nations, and
I am exalted throughout the whole earth.

PSALM 46:10 TPT

. . . .

Recognizing God is God may sound silly, but chances are we forget it from time to time. And when we do, our peace is ripped away. How does that happen? Every time we try to fix things ourselves, we're assuming the role of God. When we look for worldly solutions, we're choosing here over Him. When we expect our friends or family to bail us out of trouble, we are elevating their status above God's.

If our goal is to experience peace, then we need to experience God daily. That means understanding His vital role in our life. And as we share our anxiety through prayer, it gives God the opportunity to remind us of His goodness and glory.

What God Promises

*So don't be afraid. I am here, with you;
don't be dismayed, for I am your God. I will
strengthen you, help you. I am here with My
right hand to make right and to hold you up.*

ISAIAH 41:10 VOICE

In those moments when stress and anxiety feel overwhelming, it's vital to remember God's promises to those who love Him. Because when we do, it will usher in a peace that's beyond understanding. Let these sink into your heart right now.

Friend, the Lord is with you. Right here. Right now. He is your God, today and always. He will fill you with strength and help you navigate every struggle you are facing today, and He will provide the same tomorrow, no matter what the future might bring. God will make things right and He will hold you up through the valleys of life. You are loved. You are safe. And there is nothing that can change it.

He Will Give You Peace

The Eternal One bless and keep you. May He make His face shine upon you and be gracious to you. The Eternal lift up His countenance to look upon you and give you peace.
NUMBERS 6:24–26 VOICE

There is something powerful about the words in today's verse. It's full of hope and promise. It settles an anxious heart. It reminds us of the depth and breadth of God's love. It shows us His divine capabilities and unmatched grace. And it lets us know we are seen.

Let these truths usher in His unshakable peace to cover every worry or fear nagging at you right now. Stand confident knowing the one who made the heavens and the earth is fully engaged in your life. The one who created your person blesses you with the goodness of His presence, nonstop. He will give you the peace you so desperately crave.

A Refreshed Life

"Are you weary, carrying a heavy burden?
Come to me. I will refresh your life, for I am
your oasis. Simply join your life with mine.
Learn my ways and you'll discover that I'm
gentle, humble, easy to please. You will find
refreshment and rest in me. For all that I require
of you will be pleasant and easy to bear."

MATTHEW 11:28-30 TPT

. . . .

Sometimes we just need our life refreshed, especially when we've come out of a rough season. Be it grief, betrayal, loss, failure, or something else, there are times life kicks us in the gut. We need change—something new. We need to regroup before we can move forward in meaningful ways. And God is inviting us into His rest.

What will we find there? We'll experience His gentle handling of our broken heart. We won't feel burdened with lofty expectations. There will be peace and love and a safe place to catch our breath. And God's presence will refresh us more each day.

When God Reigns

Do not allow people to slander something you find to be good because the kingdom of God is not about eating and drinking. When God reigns, the order of the day is redeeming justice, true peace, and joy made possible by the Holy Spirit.
ROMANS 14:16–17 VOICE

Want to experience peace every day? Then make an intentional decision to let God reign in your heart. That means you focus your time and attention on His goodness over grievances with the world. You focus on His promises and not your problems. You trust His sovereignty more than your solutions. And you embrace God's will over your ways.

Friend, what changes do you need to make in your life so His peace is possible? Don't miss out on what God has available to every believer. Surrender your ideas. Be humble. And ask the Lord to reign supreme in your heart.

Recipe for Peace

Celebrate always, pray constantly, and give thanks to God no matter what circumstances you find yourself in. (This is God's will for all of you in Jesus the Anointed.) Don't suppress the Spirit. Don't downplay prophecies. Take a close look at everything, test it, then cling to what is good. Put away every form of evil.

1 Thessalonians 5:16–22 voice

. . . .

This passage of scripture is a recipe for peace in the heart of a believer. It's a road map to experience God's goodness regardless of what's happening in the world. And when you walk out its instruction, you will feel a sense of calm that's unmatched by worldly solutions.

Each time you choose to celebrate, pray, and give thanks to God, you'll be blessed. When you embrace the Spirit moving in your life, you will be blessed. When you heed wisdom and utilize discernment, you will be blessed. And in that blessing, peace comes too.

Being at Peace with God

Now be of use to God; be at peace with
Him, and goodness will return to your life.
Receive instruction directly from His lips,
and make His words a part of you. If you
return to the Highest One, you will be restored.
JOB 22:21-23 VOICE

Eliphaz the Temanite made strong suggestions to Job. This friend was calling Job higher, encouraging him to restore his faith in important ways. His hope was to see his friend refreshed and restored. And behind it was a belief that doing so would help God's goodness return to his life.

If you aren't at peace with God right now or if you've closed your life off to Him, repent and ask the Lord to be significant in your life again. Share your struggles and joys through prayer, asking for guidance each day. Then take those words and walk them out with passion and purpose. Turn back to God. He is waiting.

God's Plans for You Are Peaceful

" 'For I know the plans and thoughts that
I have for you,' says the LORD, 'plans for
peace and well-being and not for disaster,
to give you a future and a hope.' "
JEREMIAH 29:11 AMP

You may find it funny to hear that God's plans for you are peaceful—especially because your life feels anything but. Your emotions are all over the board. Your relationships are filled with drama. And it's hard to find firm footing. The truth still stands, however. God's blueprints for those who love Him are full of peace, comfort, and hope.

Consider this, friend. When you are in a right relationship with God and making choices that deepen your faith, peace will be a natural overflow from those decisions. That means even if your circumstances are messy, peace can coexist. Comfort and hope can coincide. With God, it doesn't have to be one or the other.

Peace from His Rescue

"Then you will call on Me and you will come and pray to Me, and I will hear [your voice] and I will listen to you."

JEREMIAH 29:12 AMP

Just like the Lord restored His people after being exiled in Babylon for seventy years, God will restore you too. He is in the business of freeing captives. He brings renewal in the right ways and at the right time. And when God hears His children crying out, He will respond.

Don't stay silent when your heart is stirred up with fear or worry. Don't remain quiet when you need divine intervention in your circumstances. Lift your voice in prayer and call on God to help. Whisper, speak, or yell. Just tell Him every burden sitting on your shoulders. Scripture says the Lord will listen when you do. He will hear your cry. And when He comes to your rescue, peace follows.

When You Look for God

"You will look for Me intently, and you will find Me. Yes, I will be found by you," says the Eternal, "and I will restore your fortunes and gather you from all the nations where you've been scattered—all the places where I have driven you. I will bring you back to the land that is your rightful home."

JEREMIAH 29:13-14 VOICE

Scripture is clear that when you look for God—look with all your heart—you will find Him. You don't have to go on a treasure hunt, crossing your fingers in hope of discovery. He doesn't try to hide away to frustrate His followers. And there's no luck involved. So, take a deep breath, friend. God is right here, waiting for you. There is peace in that truth, so grab it.

Regardless of what's going on, the Lord will restore. And while that may look different in each situation, His promise to lovingly insert Himself remains the same.

A Future of Peace

*Observe those who have integrity and
watch those whose heart is right because
the future belongs to persons of peace. But
wrongdoers will be destroyed all together;
the future of the wicked will be cut short.*
PSALM 37:37-38 CEB

Every day you have a choice, and it's a big one because peace is on the line. Scripture draws a stark comparison between one who values integrity and one who doesn't. There are those whose hearts are right with God and those who embrace wrongdoing. And if you're on the losing side, life won't ever be truly fulfilling. Even more, you'll never experience the peace of Jesus.

Choose to live a righteous life—a life that is right with God. Live in a way that honors His commands. Make decisions that glorify who He is in Your life. And be full of integrity so a future of peace will rightfully belong to you.

Holiness versus Happiness

Run as fast as you can from all the ambitions and lusts of youth; and chase after all that is pure. Whatever builds up your faith and deepens your love must become your holy pursuit. And live in peace with all those who worship our Lord Jesus with pure hearts.

2 TIMOTHY 2:22 TPT

With all you've got, choose holiness. Sometimes we get confused and chase after happiness instead. And if we're ever able to catch it, it's fleeting and fickle because it's often based on earthly circumstances. But scripture encourages us to pursue what is holy. Doing so deepens our love for God and others, and it matures our faith so it's unwavering.

Life is full of choices, friend. And choosing to pursue whatever builds up your faith allows peace to infiltrate the places that feel unsteady. It's hard to pick holy over happy, but when you do the blessings overflow every time.

Flavor and Peace

"Salt is excellent for seasoning. But if salt becomes tasteless, how can its flavor ever be restored? Your lives, like salt, are to season and preserve. So don't lose your flavor, and preserve the peace in your union with one another."

MARK 9:50 TPT

Once again, scripture tells us to live in peace. This consistent theme in God's Word matters, and it should catch our attention. Let's decide to make it happen whenever possible, seeking it as part of righteous living to glorify God.

But let's also remember His command to bring flavor to those relationships too. We need to stay rooted in the Word and growing in our relationship, so we don't become dull. If we back off of our faith, our witness will weaken. Our ability to be peacekeepers will plummet. And our call to flavor will fall flat. Every day, choose God and let Him sweetly season your life.

Prayerful Asking

*"This is the reason I urge you to boldly believe
for whatever you ask for in prayer—be convinced
that you have received it and it will be yours."*

MARK 11:24 TPT

. . . .

When you ask God for help, do you do so with confidence?
Do you seek Him with assurance, trusting His ability and
willingness to bless you? Is there peace in your heart
because you know God hears you and will answer? Your
heavenly Father wants you to approach His throne with
a heart of reverence and reconciliation, with courage and
certainty, as you ask with assuredness.

Friend, you can pray and experience peace as you do.
There's no good reason to be afraid of sharing your needs.
There's no reason to be timid as you ask for forgiveness.
Instead, be bold and know God will bless you in the right
ways and at the right time.

Keep Moving Forward

*So be made strong even in your weakness
by lifting up your tired hands in prayer and
worship. And strengthen your weak knees,
for as you keep walking forward on God's paths
all your stumbling ways will be divinely healed!*

Hebrews 12:12-13 TPT

The big takeaway from today's scripture reading is the need to keep moving forward regardless of the obstacles in your path. When you feel weak and ill equipped for the battle, lift your hands in prayer. When your strength is gone, worship the Lord through music and singing. Choose to rest in Him rather than sink in the chaos. Choose His peace over the fog of the personal war you're in.

Scripture says that when we keep walking, healing will come. The weight of our problems will be replaced with His peace because our faith is in motion. We'll be made strong through it. And we won't be stuck in the muck that life often brings our way. Instead, victory through the Lord will prevail.

When God Corrects

*Our parents corrected us for a time as seemed
good to them, but God only corrects us to our
good so that we may share in His holiness.
When punishment is happening, it never seems
pleasant, only painful. Later, though, it yields
the peaceful fruit called righteousness to
everyone who has been trained by it.*
HEBREWS 12:10-11 VOICE

Today's verse tells us that discipline will eventually bring peace. Doesn't that almost feel counterintuitive? The truth is that no one likes to be corrected, especially as an adult. We don't appreciate chastisement in any form. And constructive criticism isn't always constructive, right?

But God's way isn't anything like how we do things. That means we can fully trust that His plans are always for our good and His glory. And in the end, a gentle peace will settle in our heart as we realize the miraculous ways His correction has blessed us.

Peace from God

*Eternal One, You are preparing peace for us;
in fact, everything we have accomplished
has come from You. Others have tried to
rule over us, but You, Eternal One, are
our God. At the end of the day, when all
is done, we acknowledge only You.*
ISAIAH 26:12–13 VOICE

True believers have a firm understanding that God loves and cares for them. He is why they've been able to stand strong and persevere. Because of this, they're able to respond with faithfulness when faced with a fork in the road. For every situation that demands a choice be made, they follow the Lord's leading. Even when faced with oppression and opposition, those who truly love God are loyal.

It's in this pursuit of righteous living that peace thrives. It comes from Him and flows out in abundance when we stay close to the Lord. And regardless of the difficulties we face, by faith we can navigate the hard stuff from a place of peace.

Refuse to Fight

*Honor is due those who refuse to fight
at the drop of a hat, but every fool
jumps at an opportunity to quarrel.*
PROVERBS 20:3 VOICE

. . . .

It shows your good character when you're not quick to engage in a fight. It also reveals maturity of faith and godly wisdom. The Lord talks often about His desire for us to be peacemakers and peacekeepers. He wants us to live in unity, creating powerful and encouraging community with those around us. His heart is for harmony. And when we align with this hope, we delight God in countless ways.

In contrast, scripture says that when we are quick to quarrel, we are acting like a fool. It may feel good in the moment, but it tears people down. It breaks the strong bonds of our relationships. And it stirs up dissent rather than create togetherness. Friend, choose to be slow to anger and full of peace.

Moving Forward

*Every one of your children, the people who
call you home, will be students of the Eternal;
oh, they'll be so happy and live in peace! This
time, you will be founded and grounded on
right thought, speech, and action. And no
one will trouble you, abuse or oppress you;
you will know no fear and have no worries.*

Isaiah 54:13-14 voice

. . . .

In today's passage, God is talking to His covenant people reminding them that their past transgressions stay in the past. Their unfaithfulness has been forgiven and forgotten. And their future is certain because God remains true to His word. He's faithful to love them, and that promise is unshakable. God's desire is for them to align their heart with His.

Friend, this is true for you too. You can experience peace because your past stays there. The Lord is faithful and unable to break the promise to love and forgive. So repent and move on. And let your choices reflect your unity with the Father.

A Peace-Filled Home

Better is a dry morsel [of food served] with quietness and peace than a house full of feasting [served] with strife and contention.

PROVERBS 17:1 AMP

. . . .

As women of God, let's decide right here and now to be intentional in our efforts to create a peace-filled home. Whether you are single or married, a parent or not, you have the opportunity to make home a wonderful place. It can either be a safe space of refuge or a place where contention thrives. We can make it a haven or a hostile environment. It can be a place of encouragement or opposition.

Friend, choose peace whenever it's possible. Fill your house with goodwill so all that live there will be blessed by it. Let harmony reign through the hallways. Let reconciliation rest on each room. Ask the Lord to move in your heart, emphasizing the vital importance of allowing all who enter to experience peace.

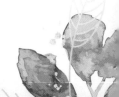

Slow Anger

*He who is slow to anger is better and
more honorable than the mighty [soldier],
and he who rules and controls his own
spirit, than he who captures a city.*
PROVERBS 16:32 AMP

When you are slow to anger, it reveals the importance of peace in your life. It shows God and others how much you value relationship. It exposes the depth of your faith because you're choosing to follow God's command more than your immediate reactions. And it is honorable.

Consider your own life and how anger manifests. We all have difficult days, exhausting situations, and unexpected moments. But when they come, how do you respond? Do you cling to the peace of Jesus or let your fear get the best of you? Do you control those fleshy reactions or unleash your wrath? Talk to God about it today and see what changes might need to be made so peace reigns supreme in your heart.

He Is Your Peace

*For He Himself is our peace and our
bond of unity. He who made both groups—
[Jews and Gentiles]—into one body and
broke down the barrier, the dividing wall
[of spiritual antagonism between us].*

EPHESIANS 2:14 AMP

. . . .

Scripture makes it clear that the Lord is why we can experience peace. It's not anything the world offers. It's not our exercise routine, our eating plan, our sleep habits, or how we attempt to maintain a stress-free life. Peace comes from Him alone.

The peace of Jesus is why we can thrive in community. It's why we can navigate the valleys of life. It's why fear can't take us out. The Lord is why we can withstand the most difficult and painful moments, rising above the anxiety. He is the reason we're able to live unoffended and be quick to forgive. He's why we can create unity with others. Each morning, ask God to fill you with peace for the day.

Eliminating the Evil

That's how you once behaved, characterized by your evil deeds. But now it's time to eliminate them from your lives once and for all—anger, fits of rage, all forms of hatred, cursing, filthy speech, and lying. Lay aside your old Adam-self with its masquerade and disguise.

COLOSSIANS 3:7-9 TPT

There is peace to be experienced when we let our old self die. It's not a physical death of our body. It's a spiritual death to our sinful nature. It's a regeneration of our spirit that happens when we accept Jesus as our personal Savior. It's choosing eternal life in heaven and accepting the gift of salvation made possible through Jesus' death on the cross.

Once that decision is made, our greatest desire should be to live at peace with God. That includes eliminating the evil ways we've entertained for too long. Moving forward, we're to choose to live in ways that glorify the Lord. And in doing so, peace will be with us every day.

Measuring Up

*In this new creation life, your nationality
makes no difference, nor your ethnicity,
education, nor economic status—they
matter nothing. For it is Christ that means
everything as he lives in every one of us!*

COLOSSIANS 3:11 TPT

We don't have to measure up in the kingdom of God. We live in a world that's always comparing and judging, but the Lord never does that. There are no set standards that divide up believers. We aren't put into categories and then assessed and evaluated. It just doesn't work that way.

Friend, let that beautiful truth settle your anxious heart today. Every bit of competition you're having to face on earth stays here. All your striving to be loved and accepted has no value in heaven. And once you choose to operate in faith, fear will flee and peace will flood your heart. Step out of the rat race and simply live knowing you are fully loved by the Father.

When Forgiving Is Hard

Tolerate the weaknesses of those in the family of faith, forgiving one another in the same way you have been graciously forgiven by Jesus Christ. If you find fault with someone, release this same gift of forgiveness to them.
COLOSSIANS 3:13 TPT

It's so easy to hold onto unforgiveness. And the truth is it's often warranted. We get hurt by those we love the most and it's difficult to reconcile at times. Chances are we've all experienced betrayal, abuse, trauma, and mean-spiritedness in the past. We've been blindsided in relationships and overlooked at work. We've been taken for granted and treated poorly. And it's left us unsettled.

Ask God to help you forgive and release offenses. They have no benefit to a believer because they rob you of peace and joy. Let Him change your heart so you're able to extend grace, even when it feels impossible.

Beginning and End

*See, I am coming soon, and I will bring My
reward with Me. I will pay back every person
according to the deeds he has done. I am
the Alpha and Omega, the First One and
the Last One, the beginning and the end.*
REVELATION 22:12–13 VOICE

Regardless of the challenges you're facing today, there's good reason to take a deep, cleansing breath. Life may be hard, and you may feel overwhelmed, but the Lord is in control. Your momentary troubles don't escape Him. And solutions are already in the works. There is no reason to abandon peace because Jesus' sovereignty covers it all.

Scripture reminds us He was first, and He will be last. He is the beginning and the end. That means He's with you always. There is no time in your life you've been alone. And there never will be. The Lord saw every day of your life before you took your first breath. Let that powerful truth soothe your anxious heart today.

Called Higher

You are always and dearly loved by God!
So robe yourself with virtues of God, since
you have been divinely chosen to be holy.
Be merciful as you endeavor to understand
others, and be compassionate, showing
kindness toward all. Be gentle and humble,
unoffendable in your patience with others.

COLOSSIANS 3:12 TPT

These are the scriptures that sometimes make us wince because we're being called higher through them. They challenge us to make choices that bless others and God. And by doing so, we're blessed too. These kinds of verses require us to be serious in our faith walk. They ask us to live with intentionality.

You know what else? When we decide to obey God, something supernatural happens. In His delight, we are filled with peace. We can sense the Lord's goodness for following His will. And while the world may disagree, deciding to love others God's way is the best way to live with passion and purpose.

Praying for Leadership

So, first and foremost, I urge God's people to
pray. They should make their requests, petitions,
and thanksgivings on behalf of all humanity.
Teach them to pray for kings (or anyone in
high places for that matter) so that we can lead
quiet, peaceful lives—reverent, godly, and holy.

1 TIMOTHY 2:1-2 VOICE

The world is a crazy place, and so much of what we experience is because of those in authority over us. While we have a voice, they have the power to bring change—good or bad. Sometimes we reap the blessings and other times we're left to navigate the consequences of their decisions. The call to pray for those in high places is a mighty one.

Prayer isn't the last option we have; it should be considered the first and best. Every day, lift them up, asking for honesty and integrity in our leaders. And as you do, you'll experience peace that won't change with the ups and downs their leadership might bring.

A Heart at Peace

Let every activity of your lives and every word that comes from your lips be drenched with the beauty of our Lord Jesus, the Anointed One. And bring your constant praise to God the Father because of what Christ has done for you!

Colossians 3:17 tpt

In every word you speak and action you take, keep it holy. Be intentional to let your life reflect your love of the Lord. The time you spend in prayer and in the Word will organically spill over into everyday moments. And it's from a heart of gratitude that you will promote God in all your ways, effortlessly.

This kind of living also comes easily from a heart that's at peace. It comes from knowing you are loved and safe and known. It radiates out from one who understands the sovereignty of God and trusts Him. Let this be how you live.

Jesus

*For God did not send the Son into the world
in order to judge (to reject, to condemn,
to pass sentence on) the world, but that
the world might find salvation and be
made safe and sound through Him.*
JOHN 3:17 AMPC

. . . .

Jesus is not just a good man. He isn't just a prophet who walked the earth. As the Son of God, Jesus had a mission to save the world. Through His death on the cross, He bridged the sin gap between us and God. Jesus came to overcome. He came to redeem. He came to save.

If you want to experience peace, Jesus is the way. Once you become a believer, your faith will keep peace activated in your heart. It will enable you to rest in the Lord even through the most chaotic times. It will anchor you to God who will strengthen you for the battle. And nothing will have the power to steal it away.

God Will Provide

"So then, forsake your worries! Why would you say, 'What will we eat?' or 'What will we drink?' or 'What will we wear?' For that is what the unbelievers chase after. Doesn't your heavenly Father already know the things your bodies require?"

MATTHEW 6:31-32 TPT

· ·

Friend, let today's scripture settle your spirit about how your needs will be met. As believers, we can fully trust God for all we need. It may not always be in the ways we ask, but we can always be assured He will take care of us. So let your prayers be a mixture of requests as well as praises for how He will provide.

Remember that anytime fear arises, it's a red flag of unbelief. It reveals that our heart isn't focused on the right things. It's proof we're not trusting God as our provider. And as we come back into alignment with truth, peace will return.

Don't Worry about Tomorrow

"So above all, constantly seek God's kingdom and his righteousness, then all these less important things will be given to you abundantly. Refuse to worry about tomorrow, but deal with each challenge that comes your way, one day at a time. Tomorrow will take care of itself."

Matthew 6:33-34 TPT

- -

When we're worried about tomorrow, we can't find peace in today. Every moment we spend anxious keeps us from experiencing all that God has for us. We won't feel settled. We won't feel confident in the Lord's goodness. And our insecurities will be triggered, making us unsure about if things will work out in the end. This isn't God's plan for our day.

Instead, when we talk to Him about every detail that brings us stress, we will find that a calmness prevails. There will be a sense that God is in control and will work all things for good. And we'll be able to keep a healthy perspective during the ups and downs, knowing He reigns supreme.

The Power of God's Presence

*You'll travel safely, you'll neither tire
nor trip. You'll take afternoon naps without
a worry, you'll enjoy a good night's sleep.
No need to panic over alarms or surprises,
or predictions that doomsday's just around
the corner, because GOD will be right there
with you; he'll keep you safe and sound.*

PROVERBS 3:23–26 MSG

- -

What a powerful reminder that God's presence is unmatched. You may not be able to see God with your eyes. You can't hug Him or sit in His lap for comfort. But make no mistake, He is with you always. In fact, God is with you right now, friend.

Why is that helpful? Scripture clearly unpacks the benefits of His holy presence, and it's available to everyone who calls Him Father. In those moments where you're feeling destabilized by life, ask God to let you experience His presence. It may manifest as strength, wisdom, or hope, or you may feel peace wash over you.

With Nothing to Fear

Clothed in strength and dignity, with nothing to fear, she smiles when she thinks about the future.
PROVERBS 31:25 VOICE

Imagine living without anything to fear. That doesn't necessarily mean hard times aren't ahead. It doesn't mean there won't be difficult seasons in relationships. There will most certainly be struggles with health, finances, and career. Disappointments and failures will happen. But when we cling to God and trust His promises, there won't be reason to fear them.

What has you worried today? Where are your anxieties anchored, friend? As a Christ-follower, you don't have to live tied to them. If you want to experience peace and freedom instead, then go to God in prayer and ask for it. Expose every hidden stress that is robbing you of joy. And find the confidence and courage to stand in His strength and boldly choose faith over fear. You've got this!

When Striving Turns Bad

And it is better to have one handful of peace than to have two hands full of hard work and a desire to catch the wind.
ECCLESIASTES 4:6 VOICE

As women, striving is often just part of our nature. We want the best marriage possible. We want to be nominated for mom-of-the-year, consecutively. We desire to appear youthful as long as possible. In our careers, we want to be the best. In our home management, our goal is to make it a loving and safe space. And while it can spur us on to new and good things, it can also keep us in the bondage of performance living.

If striving creates chaos and discontent in your heart, it's not part of God's plan. Ask Him to help you make more realistic choices that bring life and not competition. Ask for wisdom to know when you're pushing too hard or expecting too much. Ask for peace over pursing worldly standards.

The Path of Peace

Lord, so many times I fail; I fall into disgrace.
But when I trust in you, I have a strong
and glorious presence protecting and
anointing me. Forever you're all I need!

PSALM 73:26 TPT

. . . .

When you come to a crossroads, there's a choice to be made. You can lean into your own understanding and follow that path, or you can trust in God and let Him guide your next steps. You can work yourself up into a frenzy trying to figure it out, or you can rest knowing He's in control. Isn't the choice obvious?

And yes, we will fail miserably as we opt for the wrong things from time to time. We will make decisions that bring shame and guilt in painful ways. But let those times be reminders of what we don't want to do again. Because what we want in the end is to experience peace, let's choose the path that leads us there.

Welcoming

*As for the man who is a weak believer,
welcome him [into your fellowship], but not to
criticize his opinions or pass judgment on his
scruples or perplex him with discussions.*
ROMANS 14:1 AMPC

. . . .

Today's verse is yet another reminder to live at peace with one another. Are you starting to see a theme develop in God's Word? This is of the utmost importance to the Creator! And because of that, finding ways to thrive in community should be important to us too. As believers, we are so much stronger together than we are apart.

Friend, make it a priority to be open to others. Even if they're different than you are, show care and kindness anyway. Welcome with open arms and give them a place to belong. Rather than sit in judgment, choose to be one who encourages because there are enough who don't. And each time you embrace another in faith, rest assured God sees it and is well pleased.

Justified in the Standoff

*I urge you, my brothers and sisters, for the
sake of the name of our Lord Jesus Christ,
to agree to live in unity with one another and
put to rest any division that attempts to tear
you apart. Be restored as one united body
living in perfect harmony. Form a consistent
choreography among yourselves, having a
common perspective with shared values.*

1 CORINTHIANS 1:10 TPT

· ·

Putting to rest any division between you and others isn't
always easy. At times we feel justified in the standoff and
the last thing we want is to back down. We have a point to
prove. And while it may be causing problems, sometimes
being right feels more important. But friend, it's not.

God asks us to embrace unity by setting aside our
prideful moments. His plan is that we choose harmonious
living, always being willing to take a knee for the sake of
His name.

80

Just Open God's Word

All of Scripture is God-breathed; in its inspired voice, we hear useful teaching, rebuke, correction, instruction, and training for a life that is right so that God's people may be up to the task ahead and have all they need to accomplish every good work.

2 TIMOTHY 3:16–17 VOICE

When in doubt, open God's Word. When your spirit is unsure about which direction to go, seek wisdom through the scriptures. Every time you're confused by choices, see what the Bible has to say. This is how you move forward in confusing times, experiencing peace regardless of your circumstances.

You can trust God's Word. Because it is God-breathed, it will never steer you in the wrong direction. In its pages are the answers you're seeking—the ones to keep you on track with His plan for your life. And as you pursue righteousness, there will be comfort in knowing He is well pleased by your steadfast obedience.

God Is Greater

Little children (believers, dear ones), you are of God and you belong to Him and have [already] overcome them [the agents of the antichrist]; because He who is in you is greater than he (Satan) who is in the world [of sinful mankind].

1 JOHN 4:4 AMP

Take a deep, cleansing breath. Inhale truth as you exhale lies keeping your heart tangled. Let go of the issues ushering in stress. Release the anxious thoughts that have occupied your mind. Refuse to partner with the fear threatening your peace. And know that God is greater than every concern you're dealing with right now.

As believers, we have access to God's power and provision at any moment and in all situations. His Spirit lives in us, strengthening us when we need it the most. The Spirit bolsters our confidence through faith that we can stand tall against the enemy of our soul. Yes, God is greater.

You Are Chosen

*But you are a chosen people, set aside to
be a royal order of priests, a holy nation,
God's own; so that you may proclaim the
wondrous acts of the One who called you
out of inky darkness into shimmering light.*
1 PETER 2:9 VOICE

Friend, embrace the truth that you are special. Believe you are deeply loved and known. You're chosen by God Himself. And in today's passage of scripture, Peter is reiterating that fact. He's reminding the church of their value to God. As a believer, that includes you.

Yes, you are flawed and frustrating at times. You don't always have the purest motives. Your choices are sometimes questionable, and you aren't always kind and generous. But God still chooses you. He still loves you. And as you pursue righteous living, albeit imperfectly, you can rest knowing nothing can change His unconditional love for you.

Contentment through God's Presence

*Don't be obsessed with money but live
content with what you have, for you always
have God's presence. For hasn't he promised
you, "I will never leave you, never! And I
will not loosen my grip on your life!"*

HEBREWS 13:5 TPT

Scripture tells us to be content with what we have. We're to step out of the rat race and be satisfied. It doesn't mean we can't pursue being a better woman, but we can curb the obsession to keep up with the Joneses. We can recognize the gift of God's presence and all the ways it blesses us daily.

Friend, what is better than the Lord? What worldly prize can hold a candle to His promises? Don't take your eyes off God for He is who will bring deep contentment and peace to your heart. Any earthly pursuit will only create a craving that can't ever be satisfied.

Confident and Comforted

*He came to save us. It's not that we earned
it by doing good works or righteous deeds;
He came because He is merciful. He brought us
out of our old ways of living to a new beginning
through the washing of regeneration; and He
made us completely new through the Holy
Spirit, who was poured out in abundance
through Jesus the Anointed, our Savior.*

TITUS 3:5-6 VOICE

Have you felt guilt and shame from past choices? Are there
memories that haunt you? Are you embarrassed, thinking
back to your old ways? Let this stress go because your
faith in Jesus as Savior has washed it away. God no longer
looks at you and sees sin. Neither should you.

Instead, recognize you have been made completely
new. All those sinful moments don't count against you
any longer, thanks to Jesus and His finished work on the
cross. That means you can stand confident and comforted,
knowing you're fully loved and forgiven.

Through His Strength

*I know how to survive in tight situations,
and I know how to enjoy having plenty. In fact,
I have learned how to face any circumstances:
fed or hungry, with or without. I can be
content in any and every situation through the
Anointed One who is my power and strength.*

PHILIPPIANS 4:12-13 VOICE

When you choose contentment, you're choosing the path of peace. You are deciding it doesn't matter what you do or do not have because God is sovereign, and He will always take care of you. It's seeing the big picture rather than focusing on your immediate circumstances. And it signals an understanding that the world isn't your true home.

The only way we can have this kind of attitude is through the Lord's strength. On our own, it will falter. The more we invest time and energy in our personal relationship with Him, the more abundant the peace becomes.

Those Joined Together

So I'm asking you, my friends, that you be joined together in perfect unity—with one heart, one passion, and united in one love. Walk together with one harmonious purpose and you will fill my heart with unbounded joy.

PHILIPPIANS 2:2 TPT

Who are the people in life that journey with you through the ups and downs of each day? Who holds your heart, bringing encouragement to stay the course through tumultuous waves? Think of the people who depend on you for guidance—the ones who look to you for help and hope. Do you have mentors? Are you one yourself? Who are you joined together with, emotionally?

These relationships won't always be easy or perfect, but they will be vital to experiencing God's peace. Why? Because they will spur us on to seek Him first. Through them, they will remind us of His goodness. And together, we will help keep faith alive and active.

What Are You Thinking About?

Finally, brothers and sisters, fill your minds with beauty and truth. Meditate on whatever is honorable, whatever is right, whatever is pure, whatever is lovely, whatever is good, whatever is virtuous and praiseworthy. Keep to the script: whatever you learned and received and heard and saw in me—do it— and the God of peace will walk with you.

PHILIPPIANS 4:8-9 VOICE

When you're anxious, what thoughts are you entertaining in that moment? Are you focused on the *what ifs*? Is fear taking center stage? Are insecurities tangling your heart? Friend, these are the culprits stealing your peace today.

Scripture tells us to instead focus on what's right, pure, and good. It says to concentrate on what is praiseworthy. We're to think about honorable things. Being intentional in this way will help silence the worry by reminding us of God's goodness. And it will settle our heart in profound and meaningful ways, helping us experience His peace daily.

Popularity or Peace

*Be free from pride-filled opinions, for they will
only harm your cherished unity. Don't allow
self-promotion to hide in your hearts, but in
authentic humility put others first and view
others as more important than yourselves.
Abandon every display of selfishness.
Possess a greater concern for what matters
to others instead of your own interests.*

PHILIPPIANS 2:3-4 TPT

When we set aside our lofty plans for popularity, we can
relax. We can disengage because we won't have to be
working every angle to stay relevant. There will be no
good reason for tedious self-promotion, leading us to look
for ways to be better than others. Instead, we'll be free to
love others with selfless, humble hearts.

Think about the energy it takes to live with pride. It
requires us to be on task and at our best. In every moment,
we must be vigilant with how we present ourselves. Friend,
abandon this posture and choose the path that leads to
peace with the Lord.

Choosing Truth

Therefore, after you have gotten rid of
lying, each of you must tell the truth to
your neighbor because we are parts
of each other in the same body.
EPHESIANS 4:25 CEB

Talk about a peace-stealing habit! Lying works against peace in significant ways because the dishonest must keep tabs on what untruths they have told others. And each time the subject comes up, their heartbeat speeds up as they hope to remember the lies told! It's a lose-lose situation because the truth eventually floats to the surface and destroys relationships and reputations.

But when you are committed to telling the truth, it creates unity. It not only brings harmony to your heart, but also cultivates trust within your community in beautiful ways. And it allows you to work together with others, joyfully. If you want to experience peace every day, decide to be honest in every interaction. Even when you have hard things to share, you can speak truth in love.

Everyone

Scripture reassures us, "No one who trusts God like this—heart and soul—will ever regret it." It's exactly the same no matter what a person's religious background may be: the same God for all of us, acting the same incredibly generous way to everyone who calls out for help. "Everyone who calls, 'Help, God!' gets help."

ROMANS 10:13 MSG

Today's verse is a game changer for an anxious heart. Sometimes we read about God's goodness in the Bible and think it stays there. We think it was the God of yesteryear, not the God of now. But this verse debunks that faulty way of thinking.

If you need help right now, God will give it. Scripture says that everyone—*everyone*—who calls for His help will receive it. Let this truth settle your heart, fully believing God is with you and for you always. And when you're desperate for divine intervention, all you need to do is ask in faith.

The Call to Forgive Everyone

"And whenever you stand praying, if you find
that you carry something in your heart against
another person, release him and forgive
him so that your Father in heaven will also
release you and forgive you of your faults."
MARK 11:25 TPT

- -

According to scripture, we're to forgive everyone. Be it your husband, daughter, uncle, mother, teacher, coworker, friend, or a stranger on the street, we're to not hold on to offenses in our heart. Even if what they did was terrible and wrong, God wants us to live in freedom rather than hold onto unforgiveness. He wants us to extend grace like the grace He extended to us through the cross.

If you want to experience peace, it starts with releasing those hurts and hang-ups that keep your heart stirred up. Where do you need to walk this out today? Who do you need to forgive? Let this be a priority to settle right away.

The Awesomeness of God

*Don't you know, haven't you heard or even been
told from your earliest memories how the earth
came to be? Who else could have done it except
God, enthroned high above the earth? From such
a vantage people seem like grasshoppers to Him.
Who else but God could stretch out the skies as
if they were a curtain, draw them tight, suspend
them over our heads like the roof of a tent?*

ISAIAH 40:21–22 VOICE

When you're feeling anxious about certain circumstances, consider the size of our God in comparison to the size of your Goliath. Today's scripture offers a powerful reminder for all believers. While your problems may feel overwhelming at the moment—stealing every bit of joy and peace you possess—they have nothing on the Creator who is enthroned high above the earth.

Never lose sight of God's awesomeness. As you cry out to the Lord for help, God will settle your anxious heart as He shifts your situation. As a Christian, you are always in good hands.

Be a Bridge Builder

Respond gently when you are confronted and you'll defuse the rage of another. Responding with sharp, cutting words will only make it worse. Don't you know that being angry can ruin the testimony of even the wisest of men?

PROVERBS 15:1 TPT

- -

Want to experience peace in relationships? Then learn to respond gently. Too often, we react in haste and harshness. Our words are short and sharp. We're unaware of our unkind tone and increased volume. And in our angst, we only make matters worse.

God wants you to love others well. He wants you to be a bridge builder rather than one who burns them to the ground. His desire is for you to be selfless and humble, yet fierce in compassion and care. And when you choose to live in this way, you will bring peace into the mix, not only for others, but for you too.

Guard Your Heart

*So above all, guard the affections of your heart,
for they affect all that you are. Pay attention
to the welfare of your innermost being, for
from there flows the wellspring of life.*

PROVERBS 4:23 TPT

If peaceful living is your goal, then be sure to protect your heart. That means being intentional to guard your mind. It's important you're careful of what you allow yourself to see. Be sensitive to what you choose to watch and read. Be aware of the influences you let into your life because they can have a profound effect on your peace. If you're not careful, they can steal joy.

There are many moving parts in the world today, which is why the Word says to be on guard. It's not a passive command. It's an active choice we make daily—sometimes hourly. And when you remain on guard, it'll usher in God's goodness each day. Because from your heart flows the wellspring of your life.

Knowing God Is Your Source

*"I am the sprouting vine and you're my branches.
As you live in union with me as your source,
fruitfulness will stream from within you—but when
you live separated from me you are powerless."*
JOHN 15:5 TPT

- -

When we're feeling anxious, it's because we are forgetting God is our source who provides for all our needs. He is who will rescue us from difficult situations. God will be the one to make a way when there seems to be none. And when you stay connected to Him, you will experience both power and peace.

So today, choose to live in union with the Lord. Make decisions that agree with His Word. Don't stray from His will and ways. Follow His commands as you pursue righteousness. And ask for what you need each day, trusting God will give to you in abundance.

Let This Be Your Goal

Now, this is the goal: to live in harmony with one another and demonstrate affectionate love, sympathy, and kindness toward other believers. Let humility describe who you are as you dearly love one another.

1 PETER 3:8 TPT

How do you love another dearly, like today's scripture suggests? Make note of the vital role humility plays in it. It's to *describe* us—describe who we are. It's having a servant's heart rather than a selfish one. It's showing deep and affectionate love, even when it's difficult to do. Loving dearly means choosing peace over pride. Choosing sympathy over self-interest. Making every effort to be kind when being cruel and callous is easier.

Friend, the goal is to live in harmony. And the only way to do that is intentionally choosing to treat others the way God prescribes. Not only does it delight Him, but it also blesses those around you. In addition, that act of obedience benefits you in meaningful ways too.

What a Privilege

And then, after your brief suffering,
the God of all loving grace, who has called
you to share in his eternal glory in Christ,
will personally and powerfully restore you
and make you stronger than ever. Yes, he will
set you firmly in place and build you up.

1 PETER 5:10 TPT

This passage of scripture is key to a peaceful heart in the middle of messy moments. It offers the perfect prompt to stay strong, especially when you want to give up. Why? Because it brings a divine perspective of why pain and grief and hardship are not the end of the world. The truth is it's a privilege to suffer with Christ. He's *called* you to share in it with Him.

Be encouraged knowing this season isn't forever. Scripture says it's brief. Yes, you will have difficulties to navigate, but they will pass. And the Lord will ensure that you come out stronger and for the better. That's why you can experience peace through it all.

It Comes from Within

Let your true beauty come from your inner personality, not a focus on the external. For lasting beauty comes from a gentle and peaceful spirit, which is precious in God's sight and is much more important than the outward adornment of elaborate hair, jewelry, and fine clothes.

1 PETER 3:3-4 TPT

When you're feeling anxious about the way you look, worried you don't fit the world's beauty standard, be encouraged by this passage. They may say true beauty comes from your body mass index, your hair or skin, or because of a youthful appearance. But friend, that's simply not true.

Take a deep breath of truth into your lungs today, and let it settle your anxious heart. Fix your eyes on the Lord and His perfect perspective. In His economy, all that matters is the beauty that comes from within. It's lasting. It's important. And it's precious in God's sight.

The Goal Isn't to Be Better

*Work toward unity, and live in harmony with
one another. Avoid thinking you are better
than others or wiser than the rest; instead,
embrace common people and ordinary tasks.*

ROMANS 12:16 VOICE

It takes a lot of energy to feel superior because we're
always working toward that position. We can't rest in who
we are. Instead, we find ourselves fighting to stay relevant.
We look for ways to one-up others in ideas and solutions.
And it's ugly. Even more, it's keeps us from experiencing
the peace of Jesus because we're always striving for more
and better.

God is clear in His desire for us to work toward unity
and harmony. We cannot accomplish that when we decide
we're above those around us. Friend, humility is beautiful.
It promotes a peaceful heart. And it allows us to embrace
others without prejudice. Make this worthy pursuit part
of your every day.

The Call to Love

And regardless of what else you put on, wear love. It's your basic, all-purpose garment. Never be without it.
COLOSSIANS 3:14 MSG

Love is a vital component to experiencing peace. Without it, your heart is troubled and unsettled because you're often partnering with chaos. You're stirred up by the words, choices, and actions of others. And it can often lead to a spirit of judgment on your part. Rather than accept their differences, they annoy you. You can't embrace others because you're struggling to find your own sense of contentment. And in the end, the idea of loving never even crosses your mind.

The world is hard enough without adding difficulties, friend. Choose to love above all else. People don't have to be perfect or kind. They don't even have to love you back. God will enable you with great compassion regardless. And when you don't see others as competition to be conquered, you can step toward them from a place of peace.

He Will Join Together

*I pray that our God, who calls you and gives
you perseverance and encouragement, will
join all of you together to share one mind
according to Jesus the Anointed. In this unity,
you will share one voice as you glorify the
one True God, the Father of our Lord Jesus,
the Anointed One, our Liberating King.*

ROMANS 15:5–6 VOICE

It's God who will give you the timely and powerful encouragement necessary to work together in community. His heart is always for harmony with other believers! And He will create a beautiful synergy of work and worship that will bless everyone involved.

Don't stress about the details or be fearful that important connections won't be made. When God is involved, you will find yourself thriving at the right time and in the right ways. Trust Him to open doors for peace-filled unity, and then let it bless you richly!

Sweet Spots of Harmony

How truly wonderful and delightful
it is to see brothers and sisters
living together in sweet unity!
PSALM 133:1 TPT

In a world full of angst, there is nothing better than sweet spots of harmony. You may find it in your marriage or a special friendship. There may be peace as you shepherd a Bible study or lead a team at work. Maybe you experience unity with your child as you parent in a certain season. Or it could be the beautiful restoration of a relationship you thought dead.

Friend, peace in community is a blessing worth fighting for. At every turn, follow the path that leads there. You don't have to allow yourself to be stepped on like a doormat. You don't have to always be agreeable, stuffing your feelings for the sake of amity. There's no peace to be found in those places. But choose to love others well, respecting one another and adopting a servant's heart.

Given Over

They are blind to true understanding. They are strangers and aliens to the kind of life God has for them because they live in ignorance and immorality and because their hearts are cold, hard stones. And now, since they've lost all natural feelings, they have given themselves over to sensual, greedy, and reckless living. They stop at nothing to satisfy their impure appetites.

EPHESIANS 4:18-19 VOICE

If you want to experience peace, then follow God in all you do. Stick close to Him, pursuing the Lord's will at every turn. Let His ways be your guiding light. And invest your time and treasure in deepening your connection to Him. Living with this kind of intentionality will keep you focused on the right things.

On the other hand, if you give into every fleshy desire, you will be left feeling unsatisfied. Nothing of the world will bring fullness to your heart and soul like God can. And peace will continually elude you. Friend, let your faith arise!

Fatigued?

*So let's not allow ourselves to get fatigued
doing good. At the right time we will harvest
a good crop if we don't give up, or quit. Right
now, therefore, every time we get the chance, let
us work for the benefit of all, starting with the
people closest to us in the community of faith.*

GALATIANS 6:9–10 MSG

When we ask God to strengthen us for the calling placed on
our life, we'll notice a difference. There will be a supernatural energy. We will have divine wisdom and discernment.
And we won't feel dragged down in the process. God will
help us persevere as we do good on His behalf, and we'll
experience peace through it.

But when we tackle life in our own strength, it often
takes its toll. We have human limitations and hard work
often exposes those shortcomings. But there's a benefit to
staying the course and doing the work. And each step of
the way, choose to lean on God.

Try to Outdo Yourself

Be devoted to tenderly loving your fellow believers as members of one family. Try to outdo yourselves in respect and honor of one another.
ROMANS 12:10 TPT

. . . .

What a powerful call! Today's scripture issues a challenge to try and outdo your current effort to loving, respecting, and honoring others. Take a quick inventory. Friend, can you do more to show esteem? Is there room to outshine the ways you've expressed morality and integrity in relationships? Are there occasions where you can show more humility? Chances are the answer is yes.

There's a beautiful blessing from doing so that comes in the form of a peaceful spirit, especially when we go above and beyond the usual. God is honored. Others benefit. And you're able to experience peace. Take every opportunity to show care and compassion to another believer. And watch how God uses your obedience in meaningful ways.

The Judgment Seat

Who do you think you are to sit in judgment of someone else's household servant? His own master is the one to evaluate whether he succeeds or fails. And God's servants will succeed, for God's power supports them and enables them to stand.

ROMANS 14:4 TPT

Regardless of who it is, we have no right to sit in judgment of another. It's not our place. It's not our right. And when we start down this rocky road, it begins to unravel the peace we've enjoyed for so long. We turn from a love of community to a place of conflict, stirring our spirit to see the negatives in others. The judgment seat is not ours to occupy.

Instead, let's do all we can to create a haven of harmony with those around us. Let's love with abandon, overlooking shortcomings and failures. And let's choose to leave any assessment or appraisal to the Lord.

Suited in God's Armor

Finally, brothers and sisters, draw your strength and might from God. Put on the full armor of God to protect yourselves from the devil and his evil schemes.
EPHESIANS 6:10-11 VOICE

There is great purpose in suiting up in God's armor. Not only does it provide protection, but with that comes peace—peace in knowing you are safe and secure. In His great love, God wants to cover you for the battles of life. He wants to equip you to stand strong against the storms that try to pull you under. And because of God's armor, He wants you to be confident and strong every step of the way.

The devil is real and his plans, maniacal. He's on a mission to destabilize and destroy every believer. So, armor up in preparation for his evil schemes. Alone, you're a sitting duck. But when you bring God into the mix, you'll be covered in His love and peace every time.

The Power of Prayer

Pray always. Pray in the Spirit. Pray about
everything in every way you know how!
And keeping all this in mind, pray on behalf
of God's people. Keep on praying feverishly,
and be on the lookout until evil has been stayed.
EPHESIANS 6:18 VOICE

The simple truth is that prayer brings peace. When we finally go to God with what burdens our heart, the heaviness lifts and we experience a powerful calm. Our situation could still be messy. Our mind may be running ninety to nothing. And our heart may be torn in two. But we'll have a clarity of issue and a deep belief that God is in control, so we don't have to be. We'll be able to rest in truth.

No matter what circumstances are clouding your day, pray. Tell the Lord about your fears and worries. Share your anxious thoughts in earnest. Open up, letting God know what's weighing on your heart right now. For when you do, peace will ensue.

It's by Grace Alone

For it's by God's grace that you have been saved. You receive it through faith. It was not our plan or our effort. It is God's gift, pure and simple. You didn't earn it, not one of us did, so don't go around bragging that you must have done something amazing.

EPHESIANS 2:8–9 VOICE

There is peace in knowing our salvation has nothing to do with our effort. We can't be good enough for heaven. There isn't a list of to-dos we need to scratch off each day. God isn't judging our choices, keeping score, and tallying up our points. Friend, take a deep breath and thank the Lord we've been saved by grace alone.

This beautiful truth should create a peace-filled heart in every believer. It produces an attitude of gratitude. And it forms a deep love and appreciation for the Father. Today, embrace this gift and recognize His goodness.

Here for a Reason

*For we are the product of His hand,
heaven's poetry etched on lives, created
in the Anointed, Jesus, to accomplish the
good works God arranged long ago.*
EPHESIANS 2:10 VOICE

In those moments where you think you have no purpose, remember that God created you on purpose and for a purpose. Scripture says you're a product of His hand. He took time and effort to imagine you—to dream you up. And it was at this moment God also designated a future, especially tailored to the talents and skills He would bake into you.

You aren't a cosmic accident without a divine function. You're not a mistake, destined to wander aimlessly in life. Friend, take heart! Be encouraged! You were made with great intention and a decisive calling. Your life has meaning! There is a reason you're breathing air on planet Earth today. Let that powerful truth settle your heart today. You are here for a beautiful reason.

The Tendency to Be Haughty

Because of the grace allotted to me, I can respectfully tell you not to think of yourselves as being more important than you are; devote your minds to sound judgment since God has assigned to each of us a measure of faith.

ROMANS 12:3 VOICE

Chances are we've all thought ourselves more loved and admired than someone else. We have felt more special than what's reality. And it took a lot of time and effort on our part to hold that haughty opinion steady. But did we have peace too?

Peace comes from a humble heart. It's choosing to recognize our position in the world compared to the Lord's. It's knowing we are a child of God—created and chosen. And it's letting our faith be what guides us into sound judgment, so we don't misunderstand who we are and what His plan is for our life.

Asking God for Help

*Our True God, won't You judge them? We
can do nothing to stop this huge army
from attacking us; we don't know what
to do, so we are asking for Your help.*
2 CHRONICLES 20:12 VOICE

. . . .

When life feels overwhelming and you don't know what
to do next, ask God for guidance. Just ask Him to high-
light your next step. Ask for clarity. Ask Him to intervene
when necessary. And then wait for the Lord to unveil His
direction, ready to follow His lead. When you acknowledge God's sovereignty, it allows you to exhale because
you don't have to figure it all out. You can rest knowing
He has it all under control.

Let His peace reign in your life through a surrendered
heart. The Lord has your back, friend. You no longer have
to go it alone. Instead, embrace the truth that God is the
one who will always be there to help you.

No Matter What

*No matter what, make room in
your heart to love every believer.*
HEBREWS 13:1 TPT

. . . .

The call to love other believers is found throughout the Bible. Because it's mentioned in His Word, we know it's important to God. And since it holds great value to Him, it should matter to us too.

Making room in our heart to love others is not always easy to do, but scripture tells us it is necessary. It means removing any anger that continues to simmer under the surface. It requires us to do away with unforgiveness because it simply takes up too much space. And making room means we embrace God's peace and joy, letting it infiltrate the hidden places that keep us from compassion. No matter what, He is urging us to love others. It's not a mere suggestion, but a command.

Do the Right Thing

Grace arrives with its own instruction:
run away from anything that leads us away
from God; abandon the lusts and passions
of this world; live life now in this age with
awareness and self-control, doing the right
thing and keeping yourselves holy.
TITUS 2:12 VOICE

. . . .

As a believer, the Holy Spirit forever lives within us. Through Him, we're empowered to live in a right relationship with God. He's often the gentle nudge or gut feeling when we're heading down the wrong path. The Spirit acts as our conscience, helping us know right from wrong. And as we follow His lead, we'll begin to experience peace because we obeyed. We'll benefit from His pleasure.

So be quick to turn from anything leading you away from God's will. Use self-control to keep you from unholy places or activities. The Spirit will jolt and prod you, so be sensitive and pay attention. And do the right thing.

One in Mind and Heart

*All the believers were one in mind and
heart. Selfishness was not a part of their
community, for they shared everything
they had with one another.*
ACTS 4:32 TPT

There's no angst when everyone chooses to be selfless, putting aside every selfish ambition. There are no worries when a community of believers is on the same page in both mind and heart. And while issues will inevitably arise, there is no unfixable problem when the spirit of unity is at work. A divinely distributed peace will bless and benefit in powerful ways and deepen relationships with one another.

When at all possible, do life with a harmonious community of believers. They will bring life and love. They will offer timely encouragement. Friend, we need to be with like-minded friends and family. And we need to be surrounded by those who love the Lord and lean into Him every day.

Be Discerning with Community

*Arrogant know-it-alls stir up discord, but wise
men and women listen to each other's counsel.*
PROVERBS 13:10 MSG

If your goal is to experience peace, then be discerning with whom you keep as friends and companions. Depending on your company, you will inevitably be affected in either good ways or bad. Your attitude and outlook will most often reflect theirs. And since you can easily become who you hang out with, making the wrong choices carry big consequences.

Take inventory of your community. Who do you surround yourself with every day? Are they full of God's wisdom or their own? Do they seek His counsel or depend on themselves? Are they peacekeepers or bridge burners? The Lord wants us to have divine discernment with who we hang out with. Ask God to help you make any changes necessary, and trust Him to bring the right people at the right time.

Depravity or Divine?

*Don't fall in love with this corrupt world
or worship the things it can offer. Those who
love its corrupt ways don't have the Father's
love living within them. All the things the
world can offer to you—the allure of pleasure,
the passion to have things, and the pompous
sense of superiority—do not come from the
Father. These are the rotten fruits of this world.*
1 JOHN 2:15-16 VOICE

As believers, when we follow the world's path of corruption, peace will constantly elude us. No matter how we might want it, it just won't fill our heart. It can't. Why? Because true peace comes from above. And if our love of depravity overrides our love of the divine, His peace will stay at bay.

Choose today to chase after God more than any other pursuit. This world has nothing of lasting substance to offer. It cannot satisfy. And if peace is your prize, then stay focused only on the Father.

Different Functions, One Body

*For in the same way that one body has so many
different parts, each with different functions;
we, too—the many—are different parts that
form one body in the Anointed One. Each
one of us is joined with one another, and we
become together what we could not be alone.*

ROMANS 12:4-5 VOICE

There is powerful peace that flows from the body of Christ when we work together in unity. When we enthusiastically accept our differences—knowing our diverse skills are meant to combine with one another in meaningful ways—we hit a sweet spot. And when God gathers and creates a community of believers, it can be a powerhouse.

Whenever possible, choose peace. Let it be what guides your decisions, words, and actions. Make every effort to celebrate the God-given differences in others and encourage them with fervor. And watch God's goodness bless it.

The Reward of Peace

Put aside all bitterness, losing your temper, anger, shouting, and slander, along with every other evil. Be kind, compassionate, and forgiving to each other, in the same way God forgave you in Christ.
EPHESIANS 4:31-32 CEB

It's hard to experience peace when we're bitter toward others. It's tricky when we're full of anger, barking at those around us. And peace will always be difficult to hold on to when we are talking bad about others, stirred up in jealousy, and entertaining the world's evil ways. God wants all of it pushed aside so love can bloom.

Let kindness be your mantra. Choose compassion at every turn, even when it feels unwarranted. Be quick to forgive because holding on to offenses hardens your heart. And when you make the effort to prioritize these above any fleshy response, your reward will be peace. You'll experience His goodness and delight. You will enjoy sweet harmony throughout your life.

When Conflict Is Necessary

In the same way that iron sharpens iron, a
person sharpens the character of his friend.
PROVERBS 27:17 VOICE

. . . .

While peace should be our pursuit, don't forget conflict is sometimes necessary. The Bible says it offers benefits to our character. Sometimes the only way we'll make changes is through sharpening. But how we handle conflict matters.

Even in conflict, be respectful. Don't explode in hurtful ways, trying to inflict pain that matches how you're feeling in that moment. There's no reason to use words as weapons. Don't go for the jugular. Instead, choose to be measured in your responses. Prayerfully ask for guidance and wisdom right then and there. Let God give you perspective. And ask Him to settle your anxious heart so you can keep your wits about yourself. With His help, you'll find ways to navigate every struggle and skirmish with integrity and come out the better.

The Gift of Encouragement

Anxious fear brings depression, but a
life-giving word of encouragement can
do wonders to restore joy to the heart.
PROVERBS 12:25 TPT

. . . .

One of the best ways to experience peace in this life is to surround yourself with encouragers. We need to be connected to others who have godly wisdom and are willing to share when we need it. On those hard days when our heart craves affirmation, these are the people who hold us up and speak God's truth into our weary bones. And it's through their words we're able to feel peace wash over us in meaningful ways.

Not only do we need encouragers, but we also need to be encouragers for others. Community is a powerful tool from God Himself. And used correctly and with care, a life-giving word helps restore joy to a troubled heart. And peace prevails.

Unconditional Love

But God still loved us with such great love.
He is so rich in compassion and mercy. Even
when we were dead and doomed in our many
sins, he united us into the very life of Christ
and saved us by his wonderful grace!

EPHESIANS 2:4-5 TPT

Do you know why you can have peace no matter what? Because you are loved by God—unconditionally. Others may dislike you. They may be hateful and mean spirited. Your past bad decisions may be used against you. And you may feel unlovable and unwanted based on a sinful season. But nothing in your past, present, or future will be able to deter His compassion for you, friend.

The world brings much angst, doesn't it? That's why we must choose every day to walk with God. We need His care and mercy to keep us steady. We need His love to settle our anxiousness. And we need to secure our faith in salvation through Jesus Christ.

A True Way of Life

My little children, don't just talk about love as an idea or a theory. Make it your true way of life, and live in the pattern of gracious love.
1 JOHN 3:18 VOICE

. . . .

What would it look like if you looked at life through the lens of love? What if you were able to see every person the way God sees them? Rather than be at odds with one another, what if you made peace a priority with every interaction? The truth is that too often, loving others is more of an idea than a reality. But with God's help, we can walk in patterns of gracious love.

True, lasting peace and love are only attainable and sustainable through the Lord. And we owe it to ourselves and to those we care about to love well. Not only does it affirm one's heart, but it also allows a beautiful calm to rest on it.

The Storms of Guilt

There is a sure way for us to know that we belong to the truth. Even though our inner thoughts may condemn us with storms of guilt and constant reminders of our failures, we can know in our hearts that in His presence God Himself is greater than any accusation. He knows all things.

1 JOHN 3:19–20 VOICE

Guilt has a way of choking peace right out of us. When we make a mistake—even if by accident—so often our mind clings to it. We replay the scenario over and over again, beating ourselves up as we sit in condemnation.

This is where we need to activate faith and remember God is bigger than guilt. As believers, we're forgiven and redeemed. We may not be perfect, but we're perfectly loved. And when we embrace faith, a peace will settle over us. Friend, you belong to truth, which means guilt has lost its grip. Grab onto God and let His presence soothe your heart today.

When You Need Forgiving

Live creatively, friends. If someone falls into sin, forgivingly restore him, saving your critical comments for yourself. You might be needing forgiveness before the day's out. Stoop down and reach out to those who are oppressed. Share their burdens, and so complete Christ's law. If you think you are too good for that, you are badly deceived.

GALATIANS 6:1–3 MSG

Can you remember a time you were the one who needed forgiving? You were the one with the moral failure. You deeply hurt someone you love. You were the reason others got stirred up and angry. And do you also remember those who lovingly forgave you and restored relationship?

We all mess up, friend. Choose today to have compassion on others when it happens. Bring peace into the mix, offering it freely. Because while it may have been their shortcoming today, tomorrow it could easily be yours.

Stay in Your Own Lane

*Make a careful exploration of who you are
and the work you have been given, and then
sink yourself into that. Don't be impressed with
yourself. Don't compare yourself with others.
Each of you must take responsibility for doing
the creative best you can with your own life.*

GALATIANS 6:4–5 MSG

If you want to experience peace, then learn to stay in your own lane. Too often, we look at the call placed on someone else's life and begin to covet. Rather than fully embrace our own work, we crave theirs. And we decide what they do is more important, more fun, or more impressive. And it unsettles our soul.

Ask God to reignite passion for your purpose. Ask Him to rekindle your heart to follow His will for your life. And ask for courage and confidence to stay in your own lane. Then watch as fresh excitement and perfect peace wash over you.

The Domino Effect

May the God and Father of our Lord Jesus Christ be blessed! He is the compassionate Father and God of all comfort. He's the one who comforts us in all our trouble so that we can comfort other people who are in every kind of trouble. We offer the same comfort that we ourselves received from God.

2 CORINTHIANS 1:3-4 CEB

Did you notice the domino effect found in today's passage of scripture? It's such a beautiful representation of God's love for His children and community. Friend, you can be assured the Lord will always comfort those who seek Him. No matter the trouble we're battling, God will bring relief and encouragement. And as we receive from the Father, it will equip us to then comfort others with purpose.

Just as His help will bring peace, our help will do so for others. God will train us in compassion. He will show us how to care. And we will learn to live intentionally and love well.

Peace in the Valley

*Even when your path takes me through
the valley of deepest darkness, fear will
never conquer me, for you already have!
Your authority is my strength and my peace.
The comfort of your love takes away my
fear. I'll never be lonely, for you are near.*

PSALM 23:4 TPT

. . . .

What would it mean to you if fear wasn't a factor in your life? The idea is almost unbelievable, right? For many of us, fear plagues us almost daily. But with God, having peace of heart is not only believable, but promised.

Friend, no matter what valley of deepest darkness you are walking through right now, God is with you. And His authority reigns supreme. Knowing He is over it all is why you can find strength. Understanding that God's unconditional love never wavers settles your spirit. Recognizing His constant presence brings peace. Fear doesn't have to win any longer.

Let God Be Your Comfort

*Let, I pray You, Your merciful kindness and
steadfast love be for my comfort, according
to Your promise to Your servant.*

PSALM 119:76 AMPC

. . . .

What a powerful request from the psalmist, and one we'd
be wise to follow. In a world full of crazy, he knows God
will be his comfort. Be it a struggling relationship, a financial downfall, a health scare, an unforeseen accident, or a
million other things, he understands who can bring peace
to his heart. Do you?

The truth is this world offers us no lasting solution to
fear. There is no earthly remedy for insecurity. For stress
and anxiety, the world has no answers worth hearing. But
God's kindness and love are key to peace. And scripture
tells us they are promised. Be quick to ask the Lord to
meet you in those places, bringing a much-needed calm
to your heart.

God's Word Revives

*You have been reborn—not from seed
that eventually dies but from seed that
is eternal—through the word of God
that lives and endures forever.*
1 Peter 1:23 voice

Do you need your spirit to be revived with hope? With peace? With joy? With strength? Then open God's Word. Yes, it's that simple. The teachings inside were as true yesterday as they are today, and God's promises will remain true forever. Your eternal salvation is rooted in this very fact. The Bible is alive and active for believers, regardless of the issue at hand. And when you open its pages, God will meet you there. Every time.

Don't waste your time with homegrown remedies and popular opinions. They aren't worth the time and effort. Instead, go right to the Word and let God bring you hope for your weary soul. Let Him bring peace to calm your heart from every trouble.

Blessed by Mourning?

*Blessed and enviably happy [with a
happiness produced by the experience of
God's favor and especially conditioned by the
revelation of His matchless grace] are those
who mourn, for they shall be comforted!*

MATTHEW 5:4 AMPC

Loss is a hard pill to swallow. Grief from brokenness can feel overwhelming. And sadness and depression often make each day such a challenge to get through. But scripture challenges us to shift our perspective and consider those times of mourning as blessings that lead to happiness. But how is this possible?

By embracing God's love, favor, and grace when we'd rather hide under the covers and weep, we will find the comfort and courage we need to stand strong. He will soothe and console in supernatural ways, as He renews our strength. And once we feel better, we will be able to recognize His goodness and the blessing He brings.

Refocusing

He who takes refuge in the shelter of the Most High will be safe in the shadow of the Almighty. He will say to the Eternal, "My shelter, my mighty fortress, my God, I place all my trust in You."
PSALM 91:1–2 VOICE

Don't worry! Take heart! Be confident in your faith and take a deep breath. Rest in the Lord no matter what chaos surrounds you. And from today forward, choose to believe in God's promises to save and protect you. This is how you can experience peace in all things.

How does this encourage you today? Where are you challenged to refocus your thoughts? Where do you need to activate faith over fear? Let God be your shelter and fortress in every way. As you pursue peace, start by surrendering every worry. Let God carry it and bury it. It was never yours to manage in the first place.

The Promise of Protection and Rescue

For He will rescue you from the snares set by your enemies who entrap you and from deadly plagues. Like a bird protecting its young, God will cover you with His feathers, will protect you under His great wings; His faithfulness will form a shield around you, a rock-solid wall to protect you.

PSALM 91:3-4 VOICE

. . . .

When you're feeling anxious about a certain situation, remember God's promise of protection and rescue. He is fully aware of every snare and entrapment. He knows the enemy's plans. And you can rest assured the Lord has counterplans in place. He won't be bested, which means you can fully rest in Him no matter what life brings your way.

Friend, you are covered! Let that wonderful truth bring much-needed peace to your heart today. Scripture says He'll surround you with a rock-solid wall of protection. You are held!

Commanded to Guard

He will command His heavenly messengers to guard you, to keep you safe in every way. They will hold you up in their hands so that you will not crash, or fall, or even graze your foot on a stone.
PSALM 91:11–12 VOICE

- -

You are so important to the Father that He has commanded angels to guard you. He hasn't asked them to do so. He's not hoping they choose to. Instead, God has directly ordered a protection detail for the entirety of your life. Their job is to keep you safe from destruction.

It doesn't guarantee a pain-free life. The Bible is clear when it tells us that we will have trouble. But peace in those times comes from knowing we always have heavenly protection. It allows us to trust God's goodness as we walk the valleys. And it builds our faith as we watch with spiritual eyes, seeing the ways we're cared for each step of the journey.

The Reason to Cling

"Because he clings to Me in love, I will rescue him from harm; I will set him above danger. Because he has known Me by name, He will call on Me, and I will answer. I'll be with him through hard times; I'll rescue him and grant him honor."

PSALM 91:14–15 VOICE

- -

When stress and anxiety feel overwhelming, cling to the Lord. Be expectant for His peace to overwhelm you instead. Watch for His goodness to bring comfort to your weary heart. And trust God will hear every cry for help, and He will answer. Nothing can override God's love for you!

Friendships may be messy. Your marriage may be chaotic. Maybe this season of parenting is complicated. You may be facing difficulties in finances, career, and health. But holding tight to your faith and choosing to trust God will help you navigate it all with a sense of peace.

The Spirit Will Articulate

A similar thing happens when we pray.
We are weak and do not know how to pray,
so the Spirit steps in and articulates prayers
for us with groaning too profound for words.
ROMANS 8:26 VOICE

Sometimes in our anxiousness, we struggle to find the right words to pray. We become engulfed with fear and worry and can't find ways to describe our circumstances to God. And rather than rattle off the reasons we're stressed, we retreat into ourselves, unable to pray with purpose. But He always makes a way.

Friend, in those speechless moments the Holy Spirit steps in on your behalf. Because He knows the depths of your heart, the Spirit is able to clearly communicate it to God. He articulates what is weighing on you. And it frees you from having to find the words yourself. God always has your back. So let peace settle on you today, knowing the Lord is completely aware of it all.

Something Good and Wonderful

*We are confident that God is able to orchestrate
everything to work toward something good
and beautiful when we love Him and accept
His invitation to live according to His plan.*
ROMANS 8:28 VOICE

Do you ever feel like you've made a hard left turn, derailing any good progress made? Maybe you cheated on a diet or overspent on your budget. Maybe you stopped having quiet time with the Lord or quit going to church altogether. Or maybe you betrayed a friend, shared a secret, or used harmful words against someone important to you. Well, there's good news that will settle your spirit!

As you surrender and repent to God, renewing your vow to follow His plan, He is able and willing to use it all for good. He will heal and restore. He will set things right. And it will usher in something good and wonderful.

Moves In Close

*When the upright need help and cry to the
Eternal, He hears their cries and rescues them
from all of their troubles. When someone
is hurting or brokenhearted, the Eternal
moves in close and revives him in his pain.*
PSALM 34:17–18 VOICE

When you feel worried, what do you do? As fear overtakes your peace, how do you cope? Maybe you grab gobs of comfort food. Maybe you partake in some retail therapy. Do you crawl into bed and binge watch your favorite shows? Or do you run toward unhealthy crutches like alcohol to numb the stress? Friend, none of these will allow you to feel true peace.

Scripture reminds us of God's promise to hear our cries for help. Not only that, but He also guarantees a rescue from what's pulling us down. In our troubles, God comes close and revives us in supernatural ways. His presence restores peace and enables us to take the next right step.

Liberation Is Coming

*Hard times may well be the plight of
the righteous—they may often seem
overwhelmed—but the Eternal rescues the
righteous from what oppresses them.*
PSALM 34:19 VOICE

Let today's verse affirm your tough season. According to Psalm 34:19, hard times may be something we deal with regularly. Remember, the Bible flat out says we will have hard times. A life of faith isn't a cake walk. And sometimes, the situations at hand will be nothing short of overwhelming. But as believers, we have hope to hold onto.

Regardless of what you're battling, God is with you. In your oppression, He sees the ins and outs of what is happening. And as you pursue His strength, wisdom, and help, you can be assured your rescue is approaching. God will bring resolution one way or another. You can stand in joy and peace, knowing liberation is coming.

Comforted and Nursed

Heavens, raise the roof! Earth, wake the dead! Mountains, send up cheers! God has comforted his people. He has tenderly nursed his beaten-up, beaten-down people.
ISAIAH 49:13 MSG

In those moments where you feel beaten up, take heart! When you've been stomped down by life, choose to praise God for what He will do on your behalf! Learn to be expectant in faith no matter what mess you find yourself in because the Lord is faithful. And you can confidently trust in Him, letting peace reign in your heart over any sort of panic.

God is the one—if you let Him—who will comfort you in the hard moments. Your Father will lovingly nurse you back to emotional health as you rest in His presence. There may be chaos all around you, but God is greater. And that is why you can be stronger. He is the great restorer!

No Comparison

I am the One who comforts you and gives you peace. So why are you afraid of human beings? The children of men are only grass; they'll wither and die.

ISAIAH 51:12 VOICE

Today's verse offers a huge dose of perspective! As you reread, what tone is it delivered in for you? Maybe it's one of exhaustive frustration because you can't seem to grasp this concept. Maybe it comes through out of more concern for your heart. Or it could be heard as a sweet reminder that God is bigger. Regardless, the result should be peace.

Comparing the power of the Lord to humans is futile. There is simply no likeness on any level. And when we allow our heart to be unsettled by the fear of man, it usually points to a lack of faith. Today, ask for an extra measure of faith. Ask God for confidence to believe. And ask for the peace you so desperately need.

A Beautiful Eternity

*God will wipe away every tear from their eyes;
and death shall be no more, neither shall there
be anguish (sorrow and mourning) nor grief
nor pain any more, for the old conditions and
the former order of things have passed away.*

REVELATION 21:4 AMPC

When you get stressed, does it ever reduce you to tears? Does it kill your joy and rob you of happiness? Does it emotionally drain you, keeping you from thriving in life? If you answered yes, welcome to humanity! The truth is this life is hard and full of difficult moments. And they often knock us to our knees. But God has plans for our future.

As a believer, there's a beautiful eternity waiting for you. In that place, joy can't be stolen. Happiness can't be robbed. And peace will reign every day and in every way. And if you ask, God will let these be part of your days here too.

The Shattered Heart

He heals the wounds of every shattered heart.
Psalm 147:3 tpt

. . . .

Friend, how has your heart been shattered in the past? Have you recently walked through a painful divorce? Have you lost someone close, and it was hard to find your footing again? Did you face a bankruptcy that upended life as you knew it? Are you looking for a new job because you lost yours without warning? Has your child chosen a different path in life than the one you had hoped for? Did a close friend betray your trust in reckless ways?

Chances are you may have experienced that kind of pain more than once. Life never seems to play fair. And it's in those times peace is shattered as well. But God won't let your broken heart remain that way. When scripture says He will heal everyone, that includes you.

When We Fear the Future

So why would I fear the future?
Only goodness and tender love pursue
me all the days of my life. Then afterward,
when my life is through, I'll return to your
glorious presence to be forever with you!

PSALM 23:6 TPT

Few things steal our peace more than fear of the future. We become plagued by the *what ifs* of life, and it often tangles us in tight knots. Rather than enjoy the now, we wring our hands over what comes next. When we look down the road, all we see are terrible outcomes and endings. And if we were honest, we'd admit it highlights our lack of faith.

Ask the Lord for an extra measure of faith right now. Let His goodness and tender love bring comfort. Be present and enjoy the here and now rather than allow yourself to forecast a terrible tomorrow. And let the only future you focus on be a beautiful eternity with God.

145

Reviving the Weary

*Do not forget Your promise to Your servant;
through it You have given me hope. This
brings me solace in the midst of my troubles:
that Your word has revived me. Those who
are proud cruelly ridicule me, but I keep
to the steady path of Your teachings.*

PSALM 119:49–51 VOICE

In those fearful moments, open God's Word. You may not always know where to start reading, but the book of Psalms is an excellent place to start. It's written to comfort believers in the middle of trials and tribulations. It reminds us of God's promises by the telling of His goodness. And you'll experience peace as you read.

Scripture tells us the Bible has power to revive the weary. And when we camp in the Word, it will give us strength and wisdom to walk through any difficult circumstance. Friend, there is peace and comfort in its verses. So today, sit with God as you read with purpose and feel the heaviness of life wash away.

Oasis of Peace

*Yahweh is my best friend and my shepherd.
I always have more than enough. He offers
a resting place for me in his luxurious
love. His tracks take me to an oasis of
peace near the quiet brook of bliss.*

PSALM 23:1–2 TPT

When we're overwhelmed by the hard stuff, what we crave the most is a place of rest. We want to get off the roller coaster of craziness and find our footing again. And too often, we forget God's promise to lead us to the brook of bliss. It's a place of plenty. Even more, it's where we'll be comforted by the Almighty Himself.

Friend, how are you today? Are you in the middle of a joy-draining and peace-stealing season of life? Are you exhausted by recent experiences? Lean into the Lord as you follow His tracks to the oasis of peace. It's there for you.

Bringing Honor to His Name

That's where he restores and revives my life.
He opens before me the right path and leads
me along in his footsteps of righteousness
so that I can bring honor to his name.

PSALM 23:3 TPT

Because you are a Christ-follower, your life should bring honor to His name. It matters how you choose to live. And because others know you're a woman of faith, when you choose fear over faith, it speaks volumes.

This isn't a call to be perfect. But it's a reminder to live with purpose and passion. When you allow life to drag you down into hopelessness, what does that say to others? If you are full of fear and worry rather than standing in His promised peace, what is their takeaway? Be strong in the Lord, letting Him give you what is needed for today. And your faith will bless you, encourage others, and honor God.

Again and Again

*You spread out a table before me, provisions
in the midst of attack from my enemies;
You care for all my needs, anointing my
head with soothing, fragrant oil, filling my
cup again and again with Your grace.*

PSALM 23:5 VOICE

No matter what life brings your way that tries to deplete your joy and peace, God will be there to fill your cup again. Pressing into Him always guarantees abundant replenishment. Friend, you don't have to live stressed out any longer. Fear doesn't have to be a way of life. And an anxious heart doesn't have to win out. Let God soothe it all.

He is ready to bring peace and comfort to those who love Him. He is there with the provisions necessary to get though every day. Let the Lord take care of you and watch how His compassion will melt away every frustration and disappointment.

Your Focus Matters

For you, the Eternal's Word is your happiness.
It is your focus—from dusk to dawn. You are like
a tree, planted by flowing, cool streams of water
that never run dry. Your fruit ripens in its time;
your leaves never fade or curl in the summer
sun. No matter what you do, you prosper.

PSALM 1:2-3 VOICE

When your focus is on the truths found in the Bible, keeping your eyes on God over the daily grind, it will nourish you on every level. These practices will be a source of sustenance in hard moments. And they will allow you breathing room when life's stressors come into play.

Think about it. If your mind is set on God's goodness, what could steal it away? If you're full of peace-giving scripture, how could a bad day derail you? Walking closely with the Lord allows your heart to stay calm because you're expectant for the Lord to make a way through the valley.

Then Don't You Think?

*If He did not spare His own Son, but handed Him
over on our account, then don't you think that
He will graciously give us all things with Him?*
ROMANS 8:32 VOICE

There is a great explanation of God's love shared in today's verse. Short and sweet, it asks a simple question to challenge even the most mature believer. How would you respond?

God allowed Jesus to experience a brutal death so we could experience a beautiful peace. He loved us so much that nothing would stop His plan for restoration. And while He could have bridged the gap left by sin in other ways, Jesus' death was what God determined necessary. That great, selfless act should be the reminder we're completely and fully covered by His wonderful love and compassion in all ways. Don't you think God will give us all things as we place our trust in Him alone?

Secured in His Presence

*So who can separate us? What can come
between us and the love of God's Anointed?
Can troubles, hardships, persecution,
hunger, poverty, danger, or even death?
The answer is, absolutely nothing.*

ROMANS 8:35 VOICE

- -

Sometimes our peace is robbed because we're worried God will give up on us. We get tangled in all the factors that we think might disqualify us from His love. We may even create scenarios in our mind that lead to eternal separation from the Father. If that's you, let today's verse be the perfect encouragement of what is true.

Scripture—God's perfect Word—is crystal clear when it says that absolutely nothing can divorce us from the Lord. No thing and no one has that kind of power. Today, sit in this mighty truth and let it bring fresh peace into your heart. Even with all your imperfections and human limitations, as a believer you are secured in His presence from here to eternity.

No Matter the Trouble

GOD is good, a hiding place in tough times.
He recognizes and welcomes anyone looking
for help, no matter how desperate the trouble.
NAHUM 1:7 MSG

Are there some struggles you discuss with God, but others that feel too big or embarrassing to talk to Him about? Maybe you unpack worries over finances, stresses over career, and fears over the future. Maybe you give every detail regarding concerns in your marriage or friendships. And maybe you aren't shy in asking for help with parenting. But when it comes to the deeper anxiety inside, it feels too personal. Friend, God already knows it all.

Don't allow shame or guilt to rob you of the peace He can supply through prayer. Since nothing can separate you from His love, go ahead and open up in earnest. He is your hiding place. God is your help. And no matter the trouble, He is your refuge.

Pain Is Fleeting

His wrath, you see, is fleeting, but His grace lasts a lifetime. The deepest pains may linger through the night, but joy greets the soul with the smile of morning.

PSALM 30:5 VOICE

The gold nugget from today's verse is recognizing that pain is fleeting. It's not forever for believers, because there is joy to be had in the morning. But when we choose to live in defeat, pain has a way of keeping us stirred up in fear. It has a special way of beating us up emotionally, so we're flatlined and full of worry. But it only lingers for a season.

If you want to experience peace in your life, give your worries to God. Before you close your eyes at night, unpack it all with the Lord. Lay it out before Him, holding nothing back. And then let your confession bring peace as He comforts your weary heart. And when the morning comes, open your eyes with expectation and choose joy.

Who Is God for You?

I love you, Yahweh, and I'm bonded to you,
my strength! Yahweh, you're the bedrock
beneath my feet, my faith-fortress, my wonderful
deliverer, my God, my rock of rescue where none
can reach me. You're the shield around me,
the mighty power that saves me, and my high place.

PSALM 18:1–2 TPT

Anytime anxiety threatens to overwhelm your thoughts, shift them to what is true about God. It's in these times it is vital to remember who He is. We need reminders of God's greatness. And unless we grab onto these truths, we will fall prey to peace-stealing lies.

Whether your worries are about relationships, finances, health, or career, remember that God is your strength. He is your faith fortress of protection. The Lord will rescue and deliver you every time. And in His great and mighty power, He will save you—His beloved. Friend, these promises are a guarantee, so be quick to ask for help and hope when you need it.

God Always Hears You

For when the cords of death wrapped around me and torrents of destruction overwhelmed me, taking me to death's door, in my distress I cried out to you, the delivering God, and from your temple-throne you heard my troubled cry, and my sobs went right into your heart.

PSALM 18:4-6 TPT

Your cries don't escape God's ears. Somehow, supernaturally, He hears every plea from everyone, at the same time. Nobody else's prayer drowns out yours. No one's petition for peace and hope overrides yours. In His sovereignty, God understands the needs of every believer in detail and at the same time. What an unbelievable Father!

That means when you release a troubled cry to the heavens, it reaches God. He sees you and hears you. So pray away, friend! Tell the Lord what struggles are bringing you despair and discouragement. Ask for what you need. And keep nothing hidden from the one who has the power to bring change.

Mighty Waters

He rescued me from the mighty waters
and drew me to himself! Even though I was
helpless in the hands of my hateful, strong
enemy, you were good to deliver me.
PSALM 18:16–17 TPT

Friend, what *mighty waters* do you find yourself in today? Where does it feel as if you're drowning in despair and discouragement? Chances are there's plenty of places that feel tumultuous. Are the bills stacking up faster than the money is coming in to cover them? Has there been a huge breakdown in communication between you and your child? Is your marriage heading in the wrong direction and you can't seem to get it back on track? Did the treatment plan not yield the much-needed results?

Take a deep breath because you're going to be okay. God has you! He sees you. And while you might feel hopeless in the moment, peace is on the way.

You Delight God

When I was at my weakest, my enemies attacked—but the Lord held on to me. His love broke open the way, and he brought me into a beautiful, broad place. He rescued me—because his delight is in me!

PSALM 18:18–19 TPT

. . . .

Consider the beautiful truth that the Lord delights in you. Is that hard to imagine? Sometimes we look at our life—every failure and shortcoming—and decide we're unlovable. We think our imperfections disqualify us from affection and devotion. We feel unworthy of anyone's adoration, especially when it comes from a perfect and powerful God. And it robs us of peace, unsure if we're held with love and compassion by our Father.

But the reality is we *are* delightful in His eyes, and that truth is repeated in scripture. God understands the flaws that come from our humanity. He knows the places we fall short. And still. . .still, He keeps us close at all times. Trust in this and peace follows.

Nothing Can Come Between

*For I have every confidence that nothing—
not death, life, heavenly messengers, dark
spirits, the present, the future, spiritual
powers, height, depth, nor any created thing—
can come between us and the love of God
revealed in the Anointed, Jesus our Lord.*
ROMANS 8:38–39 VOICE

When you're confident in the Lord's love, it settles your spirit and calms an anxious heart. It bolsters your assurance that you're secure in Him. And it gives you courage to boldly step out in faith, knowing God is with you always.

Friend, let this truth create steadfast peace that reigns constant in your heart! Let it drive you to live your faith out loud. Step out of your comfort zone with full understanding that God won't leave you. And even when you make mistakes and choose wrongly, hold fast to the truth that there is nothing—absolutely nothing—that has the power to come between you and the Father.

The Wraparound God

Yahweh, what a perfect God you are!
All Yahweh's promises have proven true.
What a secure shelter for all those who turn to
hide themselves in you, the wraparound God.

PSALM 18:30 TPT

Where are you struggling today? What is causing unrest in your heart? Have you talked to God about it? He is waiting to hear from you. Be it strife in your marriage, a fight with a friend, parenting problems, deep insecurities, fear of the future, or ruthless worries over finances, He promises to be your covering. He'll make your heart peaceful. And with God's perfect track record in your life, you can trust He will do this again.

When you feel unsheltered and exposed, ask the wrapround God to make His presence known. Ask Him to cover you in meaningful ways so it brings comfort. You may not be able to physically see or feel God, but He can supernaturally meet your every need. And He will.

Ascending to the Highest Peaks

God, you have wrapped me in power and made my way perfect. Through you I ascend to the highest peaks to stand strong and secure in you.

PSALM 18:32-33 TPT

Too often, we get caught up in the muck and mire of our situation. We allow our problems to bring us down. We feel weighted by worry, unable to manage on our own. And the truth is, we're not supposed to. Sometimes the best thing we can do is rise above it all.

Friend, stay close to God. Seek His presence daily. And let Him be part of the ups and downs you experience. Why? Because as you invite God into each moment, He responds in the right ways and at the right time. He's why you can ascend to the highest peaks, able to look on your difficult circumstances with new perspective. He is why you're strengthened to experience peace in the pandemonium.

You Are Free

You empower me for victory with your wraparound presence. Your power within makes me strong to subdue. By stooping down in gentleness, you made me great! You've set me free, and now I'm standing complete, ready to fight some more!

PSALM 18:35–36 TPT

One of the most beautiful promises of God is the gift of freedom. Yes, as a Christ-follower we've received salvation that has freed us from the eternal consequences of sin, but do you experience freedom in other areas? Does faith galvanize you to stand strong?

Friend, let God empower you for victory through His presence. When He does, it allows you the strength and wisdom to take the next step in each battle. It bolsters your resolve to do something to make your situation better. And it allows you to experience peace because you are partnering with the one who has it all under control.

Why Trusting Is a Game Changer

But those who trust in the Eternal One will regain their strength. They will soar on wings as eagles. They will run—never winded, never weary. They will walk—never tired, never faint.
ISAIAH 40:31 VOICE

Do you ever feel anxious because you are out of strength? You may *want* to keep navigating the hard moments and see the *need* to stay engaged, but you simply don't have the emotional bandwidth to do so. And in the lacking, you're left stressed out, which shuts you down.

Scripture says that our choice to trust God when life punches us in the gut is a game changer because it strengthens like nothing else. That simple act of faith (which is not always so simple) emboldens and energizes us to stay present. We won't feel overwhelmed by the situation at hand. And in His goodness, God will replace anxiousness with assurance that He will be exactly what we need Him to be in our circumstances.

A Powerful Place of Refuge

God, you're such a safe and powerful place to find refuge! You're a proven help in time of trouble—more than enough and always available whenever I need you.

PSALM 46:1 TPT

When anxiety hits hard, you want immediate relief. You don't want to sit in worry and fear because anxiety festers. And it sucks every bit of peace and joy from your heart. Instead of thriving in life, you find yourself diving into the pit of despair. But there is hope!

When the Word says God is a safe and powerful place of refuge, it's telling truth. The psalmist is speaking from experience. He knows because the Lord has proven it in his life in the past. Chances are you've had the same thing happen. You can look back and see His proven track record manifested in meaningful ways too. So let that be what drives you to God again whenever you need help. And watch as peace follows.

164

A Fortress of Protection

*The Eternal is my light amidst my darkness
and my rescue in times of trouble. So whom
shall I fear? He surrounds me with a fortress of
protection. So nothing should cause me alarm.*

PSALM 27:1 VOICE

If you want to experience peace in times of trouble, ask
God to be the fortress of protection that surrounds you.
Can you imagine that in your mind's eye? You are standing
tall, surrounded by the presence of God. Even though the
chaos of life beats against the walls, you're safe. Sheltered.
And because of it, your heart is at peace.

Friend, this can be your reality. It may sound like a
pie-in-the-sky hope, but when you allow God to intervene
and rescue you, it changes things. Why not let Him be
the one to keep you safeguarded? This is called faith, and
it's what will calm your anxious heart and strengthen your
resolve to trust.

Confident Faith

Do not let your heart be troubled (afraid, cowardly). Believe [confidently] in God and trust in Him, [have faith, hold on to it, rely on it, keep going and] believe also in Me.

JOHN 14:1 AMP

Confident faith is not easy to walk out because life is a roller coaster. It's full of ups and downs and sharps turns, all while going ninety miles an hour. And while we may be full of faith one minute, it doesn't take much to throw us into fear. The truth is we can sometimes go from confident to cowardly in a moment.

When the psalmist encourages us to trust God and rely on His hand to move on our behalf, we should take notice. It's sound advice to live by because we know He's faithful to those who love Him. And when we forget, let's be quick to ask for an extra measure of belief so we can live in victory and not as a victim.

Encourage and Comfort in Community

Therefore encourage and comfort one another and build up one another, just as you are doing.
1 THESSALONIANS 5:11 AMP

One of the best ways to experience peace is through community. Few things are better than coffee with a good friend who builds you up or dinner with family, letting them speak encouragement into your weary heart. God uses others to provide comfort. It's in their kindness and generous spirit we often find the strength to take the next step. And it's beautiful.

Make sure you're not only on the receiving end of community support but that you're supporting others as well. Be quick to step out and love on those around you too. Be the voice of hope, helping them see the promises of God. Point out the positives. Share your personal testimony of His goodness in your own circumstances. And build each other continually as you journey together through life.

Bravery and Strength through Faith

"I've commanded you to be brave and strong, haven't I? Don't be alarmed or terrified, because the LORD your God is with you wherever you go."
JOSHUA 1:9 CEB

God's constant presence should make us brave to weather any storm. Being surrounded by Him 24-7, 365 should be what strengthens us to soldier on through the hard times. With Him near, our heart should be at peace regardless of what's happening around us. Our faith should bring a sense of calm, allowing us to navigate any difficulty with confidence.

If this doesn't describe you today, talk to God about it. Ask Him to reveal where the disconnect may lie. Ask for insight to know where your faith is shaky. Let Him open your eyes to see what needs to change. Because, friend, God commands bravery and strength through faith. And when you ask for His help, He will make you brave.

Unchangeable

The grass withers, the flower fades as
the breath of the Eternal One blows away.
People are no different from grass. The grass
withers, the flower fades; nothing lasts except
the word of our God. It will stand forever.

ISAIAH 40:7-8 VOICE

. . . .

The Word of God has and will continue to withstand the test of time. While written thousands of years ago, it's still relevant today. Social trends may come and go. The economy will ebb and flow. And life will cycle, just as it has since the beginning of time. But the Bible remains the same through it all.

Let that bring peace to your heart. In a world full of changes, the power of His Word never does. Its consistency is sweet. The wisdom is timeless. And in its pages, you will find answers to every issue that faces you today. God is someone to cling to in the chaos because He's unshakable. And like His Word, He's unchangeable. Today, let that bless you.

When Trust Feels Too Hard

Trust in the Lord completely, and do not rely on your own opinions. With all your heart rely on him to guide you, and he will lead you in every decision you make. Become intimate with him in whatever you do, and he will lead you wherever you go.

PROVERBS 3:5-6 TPT

What keeps you from trusting God completely? Maybe your father was unloving, leaving you to assume your heavenly Father to be the same. Maybe a friend shared your secret and broke your heart. Maybe your husband's moral failure caused the divorce. Once broken, trust is hard to rebuild.

But that's what faith is all about. It's choosing to trust again. This time, however, you're placing faith in a perfect God who never disappoints. He's incapable of lying or deceiving. And your best is always His top priority. Ask Him to heal your heart and instill peace so you're able to follow His lead with wonderful expectation.

God's Wisdom Is Superior

*Don't think for a moment that you know it all,
for wisdom comes when you adore him with
undivided devotion and avoid everything
that's wrong. Then you will find the healing
refreshment your body and spirit long for.*

PROVERBS 3:7-8 TPT

Every day, we have to decide to follow the Lord's ways. It's not a salvation issue because that's settled once and for all when we accept Jesus as our Savior. But daily, we must choose to follow God's will for our life. It's up to us to walk out the plan He's made. And as we spend time in the Word and understand His expectations for believers, we'll have the understanding in place to live righteously. And it's in this kind of intentional living we will experience His peace and healing.

We may be smart and have a good moral compass, but our wisdom doesn't come close to God's. Even when we feel confident in our decisions, we need God to confirm them.

Fear Does Not Come from God

For God will never give you the spirit of
fear, but the Holy Spirit who gives you
mighty power, love, and self-control.
2 TIMOTHY 1:7 TPT

- -

When fear begins to invade your heart and mind, let it be a red flag. The Word is crystal clear when it says fear is *not* from God. He'll never use it against you. It's not in His playbook for believers. So, whenever our spirit is unsettled and we're afraid, let's consider the evil forces at play.

Peace comes when we reject fear and instead embrace the power, love, and self-control given to us by the Spirit. Doing so emboldens us to stand strong in our faith. And rather than sinking in worry and anxiety, we grab hold of the gifts available to us. We choose to trust the Lord. Friend, where do you need to walk this out in your life today?

In the Presence of Others

*Then Moses summoned Joshua. He said
to him with all Israel watching, "Be strong.
Take courage. You will enter the land with
this people, this land that GOD promised
their ancestors that he'd give them. You will
make them the proud possessors of it. GOD
is striding ahead of you. He's right there with
you. He won't let you down; he won't leave
you. Don't be intimidated. Don't worry."*

DEUTERONOMY 31:7–8 MSG

Just like Moses did to Joshua, there may be times we're
to encourage someone in the presence of others. Moses
could have shared these thoughts one-on-one, but he saw
value in the entire nation participating. It not only affirmed
Joshua, but Israel too. And in every heart, peace had the
chance to reign.

Including community in specific moments can be
powerful on many levels. It's a great way to set the tone,
create unity, or bring accountability. Listen for God's
leading so you'll know when to encourage in private or
when to include others.

God Watches Over Them Now

*Precious [and of great consequence] in
the sight of the LORD Is the death of His
godly ones [so He watches over them].*
PSALM 116:15 AMP

Some of our greatest moments of peace come from knowing those we've lost are safe in God's hands. When salvation is secured in the Lord, there is a beautiful promise of eternity where pain and disease are no more. And because we can no longer care for them here on earth, what a gift of peace to know He now watches over them. Scripture says they are precious in His sight. Let that bring comfort to your grieving heart today.

Maybe you lost someone to cancer. Maybe it was a tragic accident that came too soon. Maybe the treatment plan didn't go as planned. Or maybe they took their own life. Regardless, as a believer, they are in God's capable and loving hands right now. They have His full attention and care.

Reminding Yourself

GOD's loyal love couldn't have run out,
his merciful love couldn't have dried up.
They're created new every morning.
How great your faithfulness! I'm sticking with
GOD (I say it over and over). He's all I've got left.

LAMENTATIONS 3:22–24 MSG

In those moments where anxiety is high, remind yourself of His goodness. So often, learning comes from hearing. When you tell yourself that *God has me* or that *He is on the throne*, it brings peace. Recounting times He showed up in your situation and talking through the divine details can bring much-needed encouragement. And sometimes we need to say out loud that we are faithful followers who will wait on the Lord.

Be kind to yourself, friend. Don't ignore opportunities to encourage yourself when no one else is around. Use your voice and declare His goodness in your life. Verbalize His faithfulness. And utter your gratitude. It will comfort your soul.

175

Peace When You Seek

*Seek the Lord and His strength;
yearn for and seek His face and
to be in His presence continually!*
1 CHRONICLES 16:11 AMPC

We'll experience peace regularly when we seek the Lord's presence continually. In today's world, there is simply no other way we can have a quiet heart. Between a divided nation, an ever-changing economy, and world angst, how can we be hopeful? We're facing physical ailments and diseases. We suffer great losses across the board. And we have to navigate the ebbs and flows that come with relationships, finances, and career. If we're not seeking God and His strength daily, we're toast. Peace will only be a wish and not a reality.

How are you, friend? How's your heart right now? Why not spend time in the Lord's presence, asking for hope and serenity? Seek His face, staying focused on His promises rather than the circumstances that feel overwhelming.

The Need to Belong

If we live, we live to the Lord, and if we die,
we die to the Lord. So then, whether we
live or we die, we belong to the Lord.
ROMANS 14:8 AMPC

As women, we have a strong desire to belong. We want to be wanted. We crave meaningful community where our presence matters. And sometimes we make the wrong choices trying to fit into the wrong places. In our desperation, we compromise so we can be acknowledged. The truth is the need to be known and loved is a powerful force that will lead us astray unless we find our purpose and identity in the Lord. And friend, He is ready to affirm you in every way needed.

Scripture always settles a restless spirit, and when it tells you that you belong to God no matter what. . .you can exhale a sigh of relief. You do belong. You have value. And you are fully loved by the Creator.

Now and Then

I have asked one thing from the LORD—it's all I seek: to live in the LORD's house all the days of my life, seeing the LORD's beauty and constantly adoring his temple. Because he will shelter me in his own dwelling during troubling times; he will hide me in a secret place in his own tent; he will set me up high, safe on a rock.

PSALM 27:4-5 CEB

When the world feels out of control, keep focused on eternity. In times where it seems life is spiraling out of control, remember here and now are but a breath compared to forever in His presence. Let this truth be a calming force in your heart.

Not only will God provide a beautiful and secure place in eternity, but He'll also shelter you right now when you need it. He will hide you in a secret space, so you feel safe. And the Lord will lift you above today's circumstances so you can be at peace.

Unmatched Compassion

You've kept track of all my wandering and my weeping. You've stored my many tears in your bottle—not one will be lost. For they are all recorded in your book of remembrance.

PSALM 56:8 TPT

What a loving Father! To understand His great compassion for you can often be overwhelming because it's unmatched in the world. Even those who purpose to love you well can't come close to the love of God. If peace is what you're after, today's verse comes in hot, bringing truth about your great worth to God. Let it settle over you today and reveal the importance you hold in His eyes.

Friend, when you feel unseen and unloved here on earth, refocus on how God feels about you instead. He has seen every tear and collected them. Even more, He has written down each moment for safe keeping. Yes, God's love and compassion are unmatched indeed.

Encouraged by God

Our Lord Jesus Christ himself and God our Father loved us and through grace gave us eternal comfort and a good hope. May he encourage your hearts and give you strength in every good thing you do or say.

2 THESSALONIANS 2:16–17 CEB

Don't worry. God will bring the right encouragement at the right time. He knows what you need and won't leave you lacking. Even when you're feeling weak or ill equipped, He will strengthen your resolve to take the next step forward. And you will find the energy to complete the task God's called you to.

Today, be comforted in knowing His presence is with you always. When you need the perfect words, you will have them. When you need His wisdom and guidance in situations, God will give them. And in the end, rest knowing you'll be in eternity because of His love and grace.

Your Weakness Is His Opportunity

He said to me, "My grace is enough for you, because power is made perfect in weakness." So I'll gladly spend my time bragging about my weaknesses so that Christ's power can rest on me.

2 CORINTHIANS 12:9 CEB

. . . .

We stress out about our weaknesses because we think they make us *less than* others. We decide we're not good enough because we can't cook or host like she can. We don't have the unlimited stamina or motivation like they do. We're not as trendy as those girls. And our marriage isn't thriving like theirs is. And those deep insecurities drain every ounce of peace from our heart.

Paul learned to see his weaknesses as opportunities to showcase God's strength through him. What if you chose to follow Paul's lead? It's okay that you aren't strong in every way. Let those places be where others see God's goodness. There will be so much peace in it!

Scripture Index

NEW TESTAMENT

About the Author

Carey Scott is an author, speaker, and certified biblical life coach who's honest about her walk with the Lord—stumbles, fumbles, and all. With authenticity and humor, she challenges women to be real, not perfect, and reminds them to trust God as their source above all else. Carey lives in Colorado with her two kids who give her plenty of material for writing and speaking. She's surrounded by a wonderful family and group of friends who keep her motivated, real, and humble. You can find her at CareyScott.org.